Read What Others Are Saying About Peter Manik And His Art:

"One of the most versatile and complex artists of our times, creating beauty with a twist...captivating work that only Mr. Manik can express through his photography, and through his collaboration with his wonderful models.

- Alan Pedroso, photographer artist - Miami, Florida

"I have "practiced" photography for over 40 years. I have experienced much, and I have learned much. A while back, I met Peter Manik. I have come to know him and to appreciate his amazing talent and character. I can say with a strong conviction, that I have learned more since meeting Peter, than I had in all the years before. His honest, intelligent and forthright critique of my work, has inspired me to reach for things I once did not even consider. That, in a nutshell, is Peter Manik. Inspirational !!!"

- D.E. "Darryl" Kincaid, photographer artist - Tucson,Arizona

GLAMOURHORROR

By Peter Manik and Alane Deviare

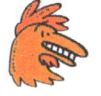

Goofy Rooster Publishing
Wylie, Texas
www.goofyrooster-publishing.com

GlamourHorror

By Peter Manik and Alane Deviare

Goofy Rooster Publishing   PO Box 2904 Wylie, Texas 75098
www.goofyrooster-publishing.com

ISBN-10: 0-9843940-0-1

ISBN-13: 978-0-9843940-0-5

Contents

Introduction

Beauty and perfection is a universal desire. The media hypnotizes us with glamorous images and keeps us hungry for an unreachable ideal.

Alane and I wanted to challenge this perfection. We injected gross horror into otherwise beautiful images, in order to question the concept of glamour. Perception filters beauty. What allures one, repulses another. The standards of attractiveness vary across culture, religion, and even mutates within ourselves.

We encourage you to take a look at these images and think about your own contrasting beliefs about idealistic beauty. Perhaps you too will find that beauty is, in fact, in the eye of the beholder.

Peter Manik and Alane Deviare

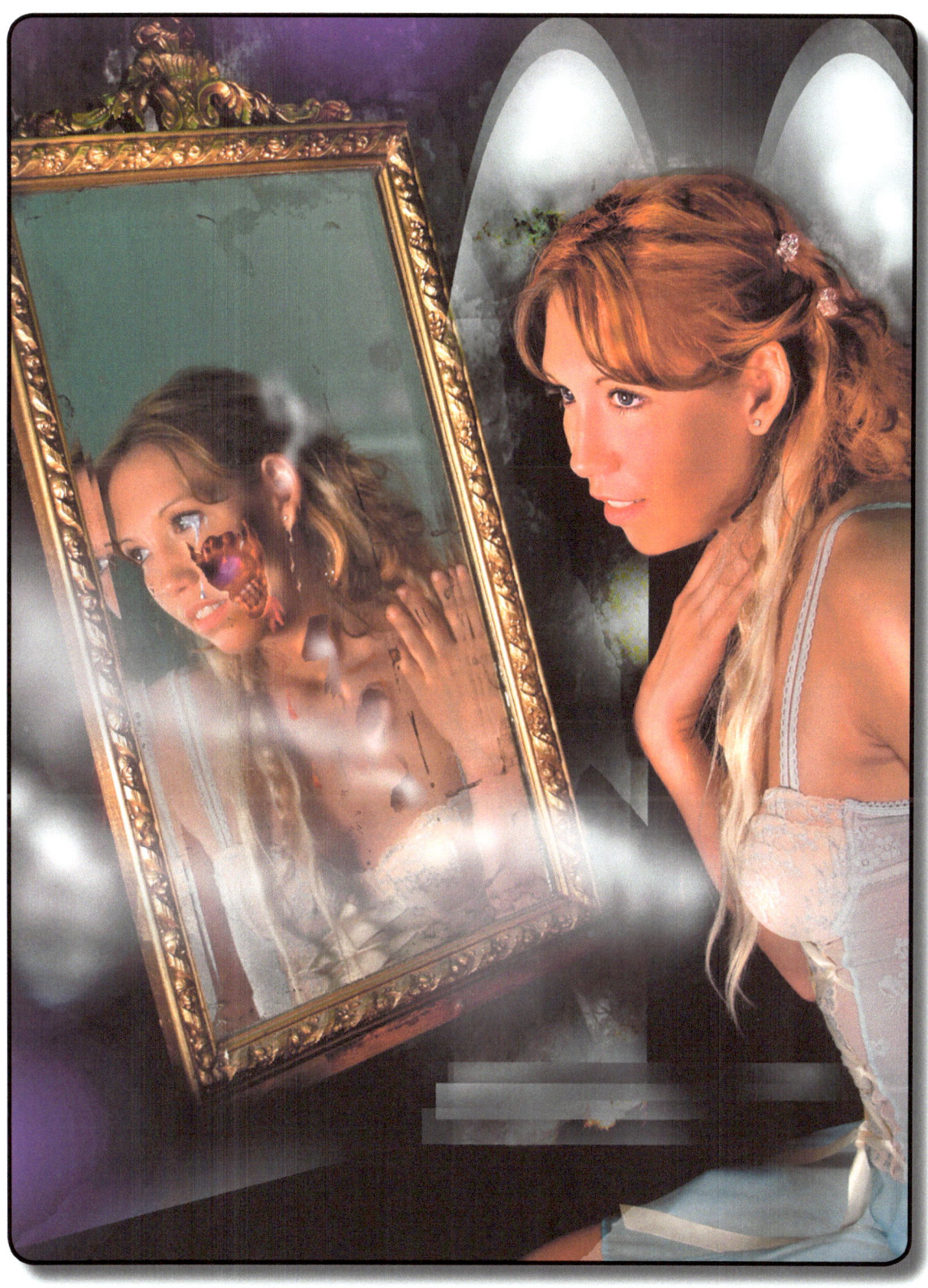

The two sides of us

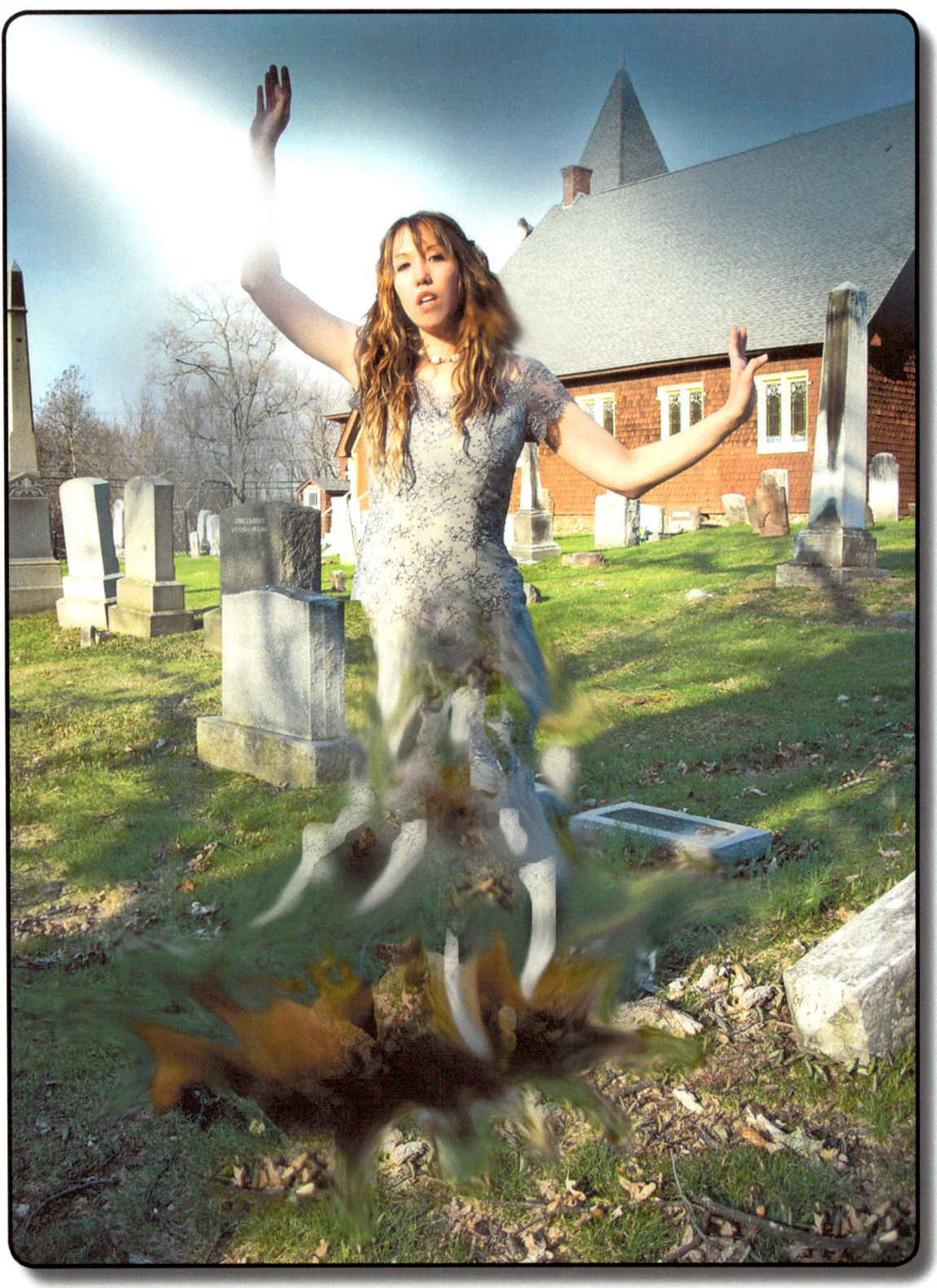

Second chance

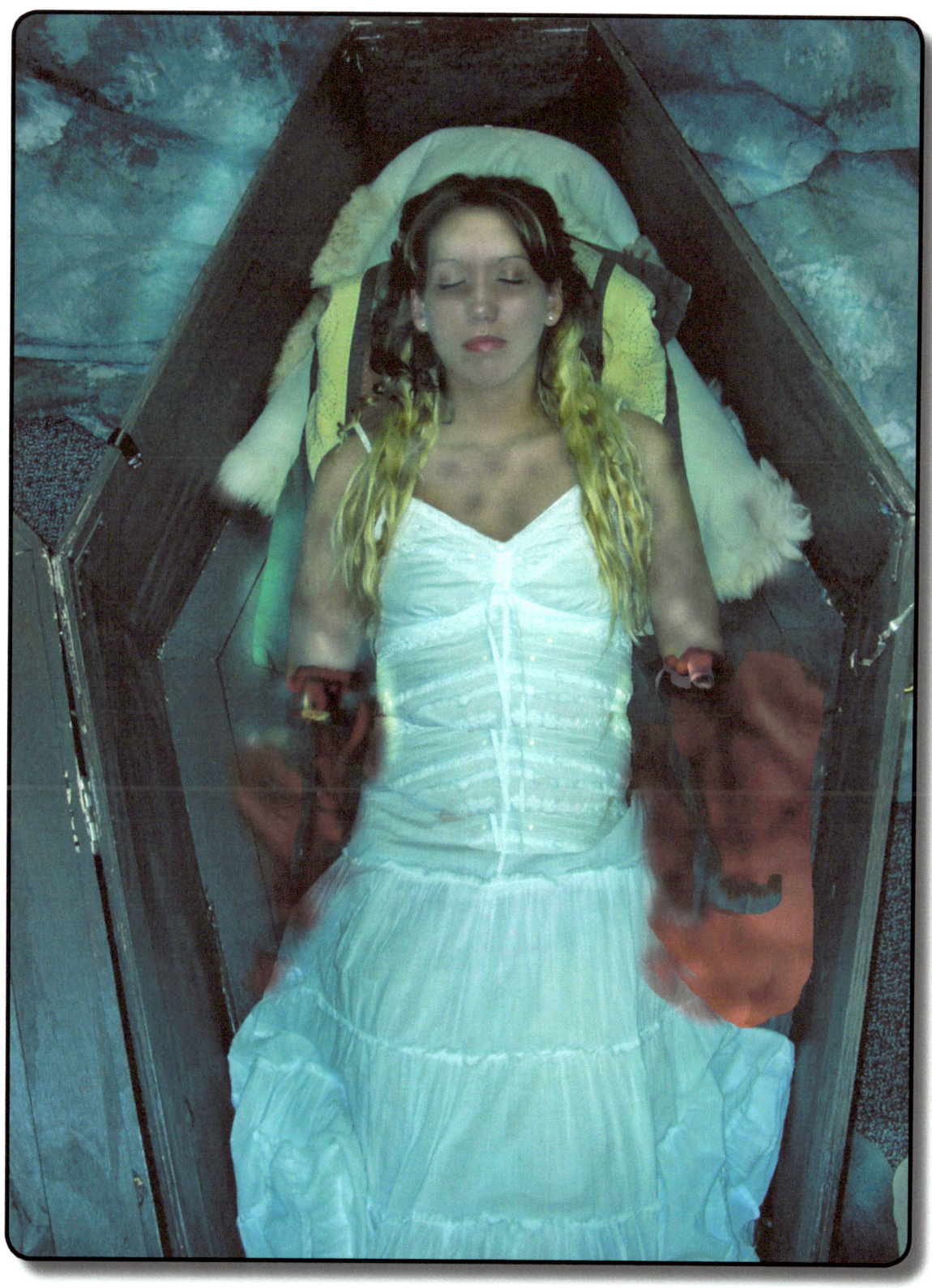

Pros and cons of untouchable

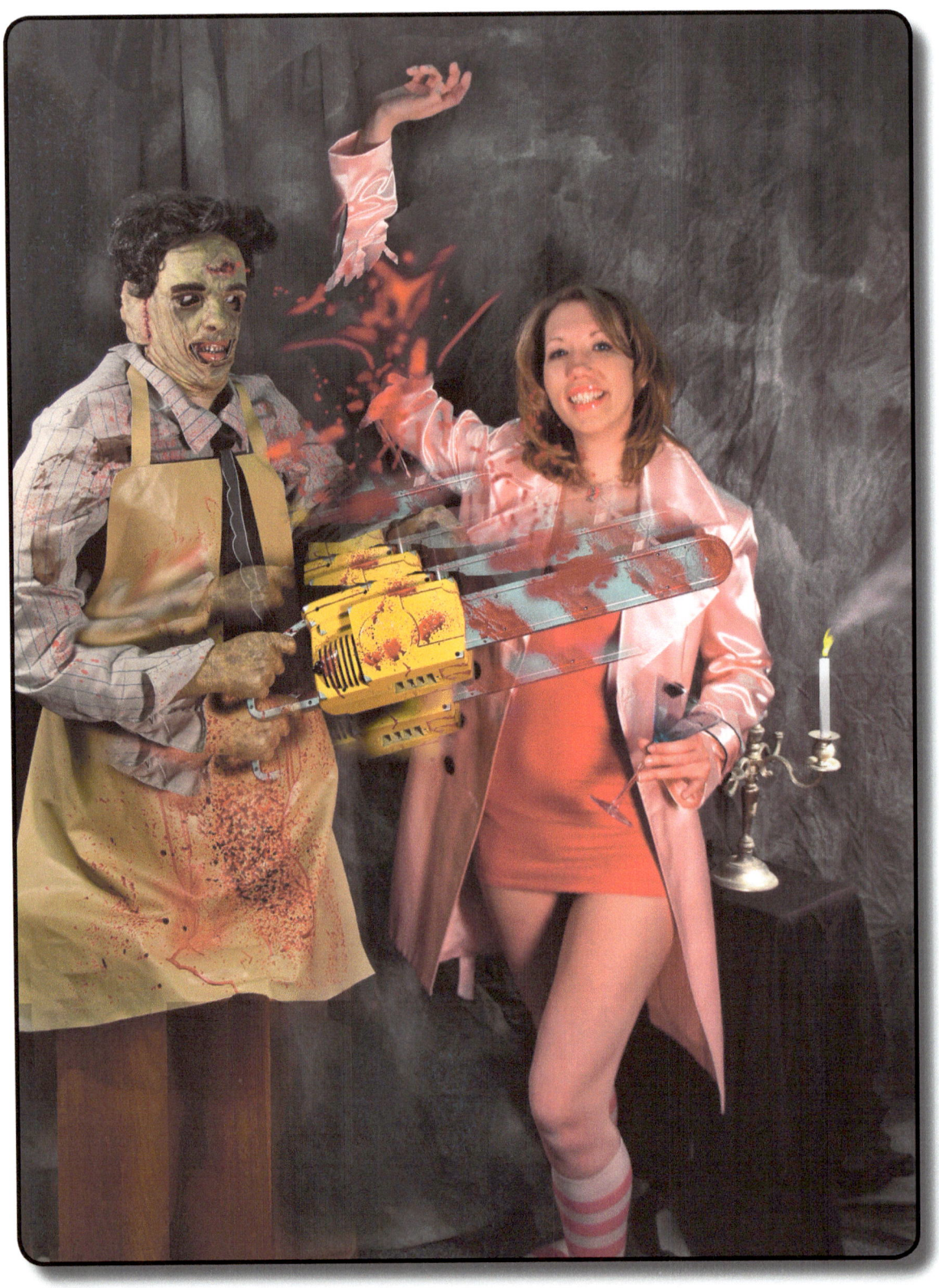

It's always good to have a sense of humor

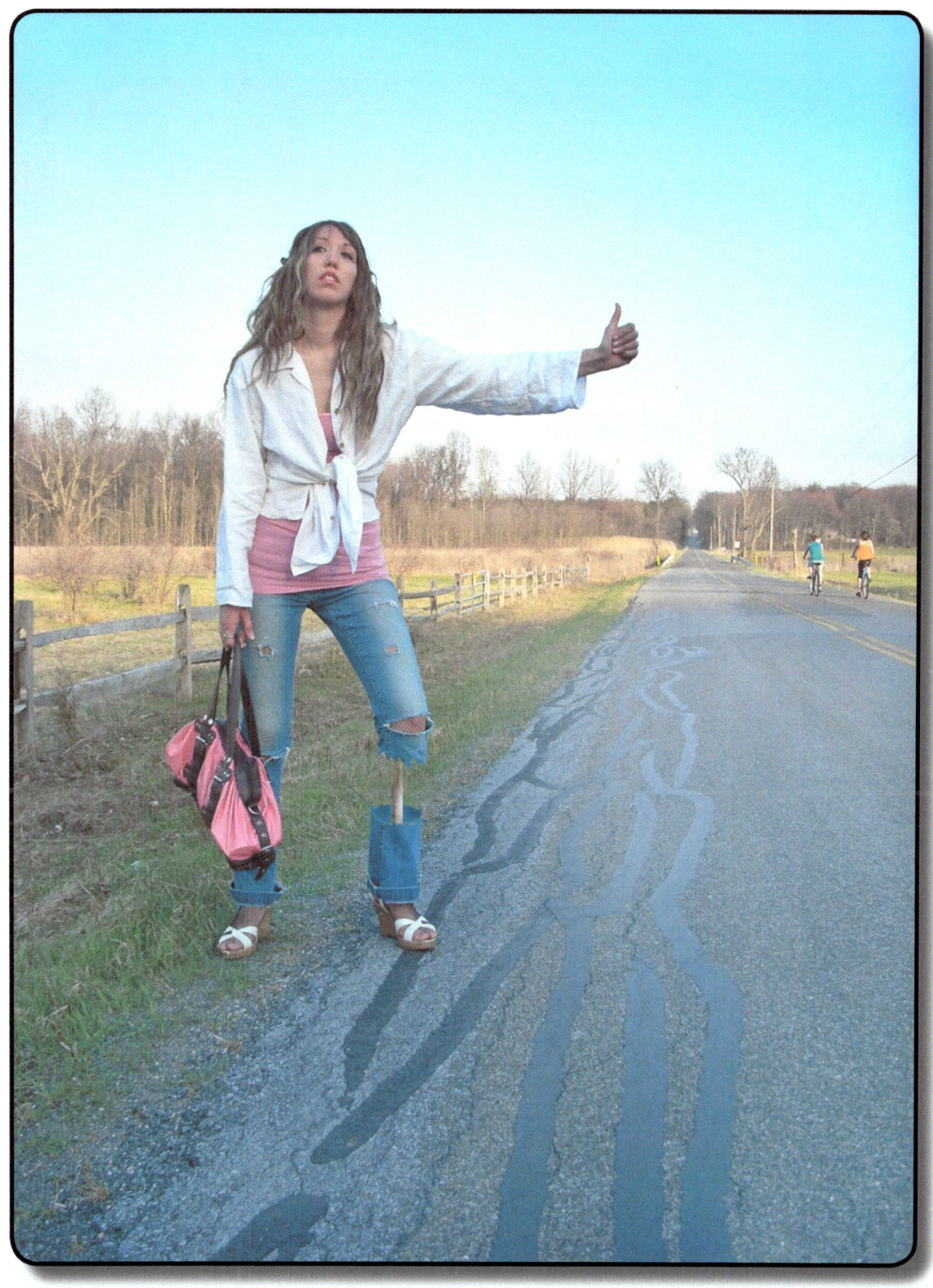

The long road ahead

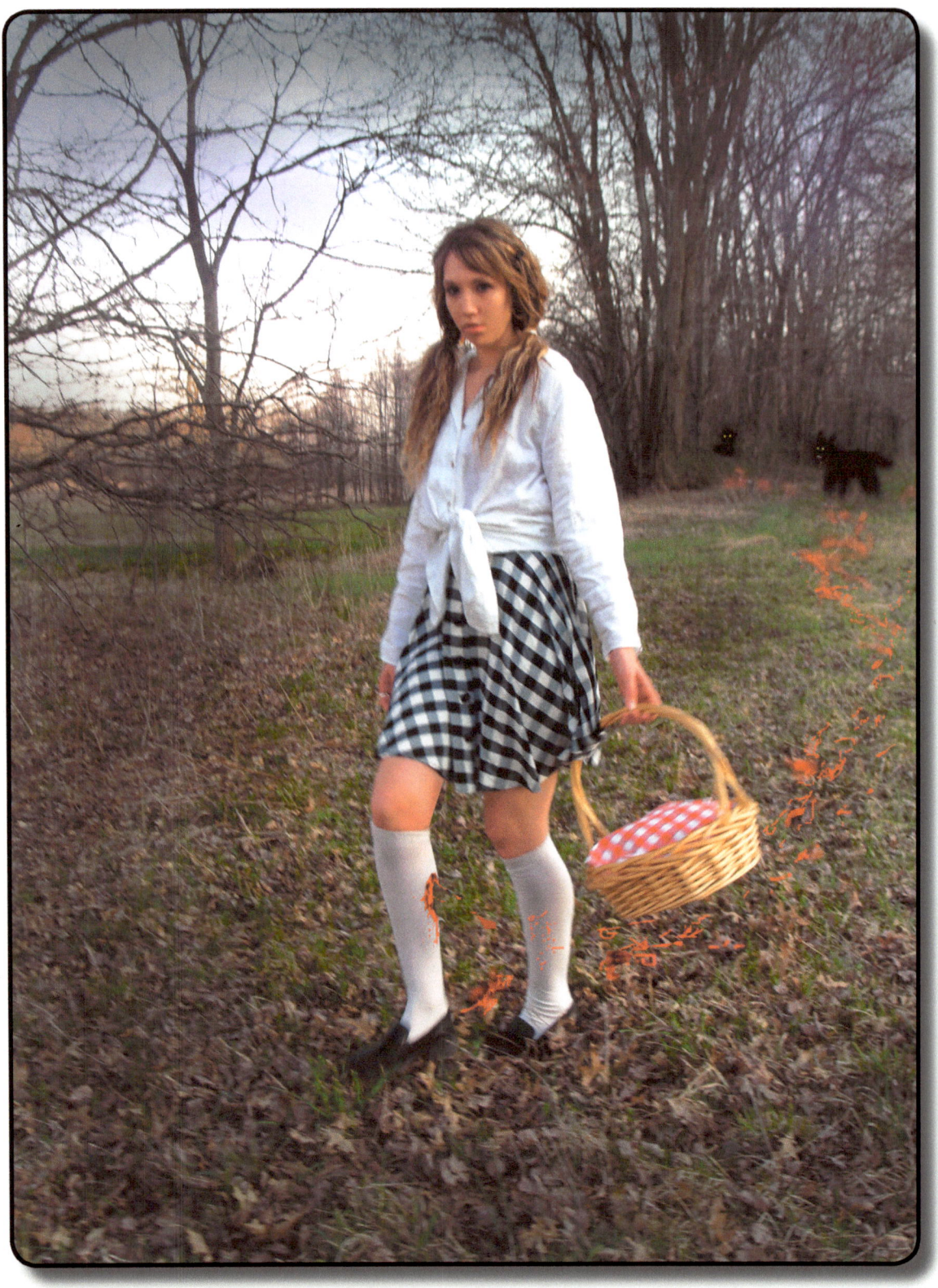

Little gray bitten hood

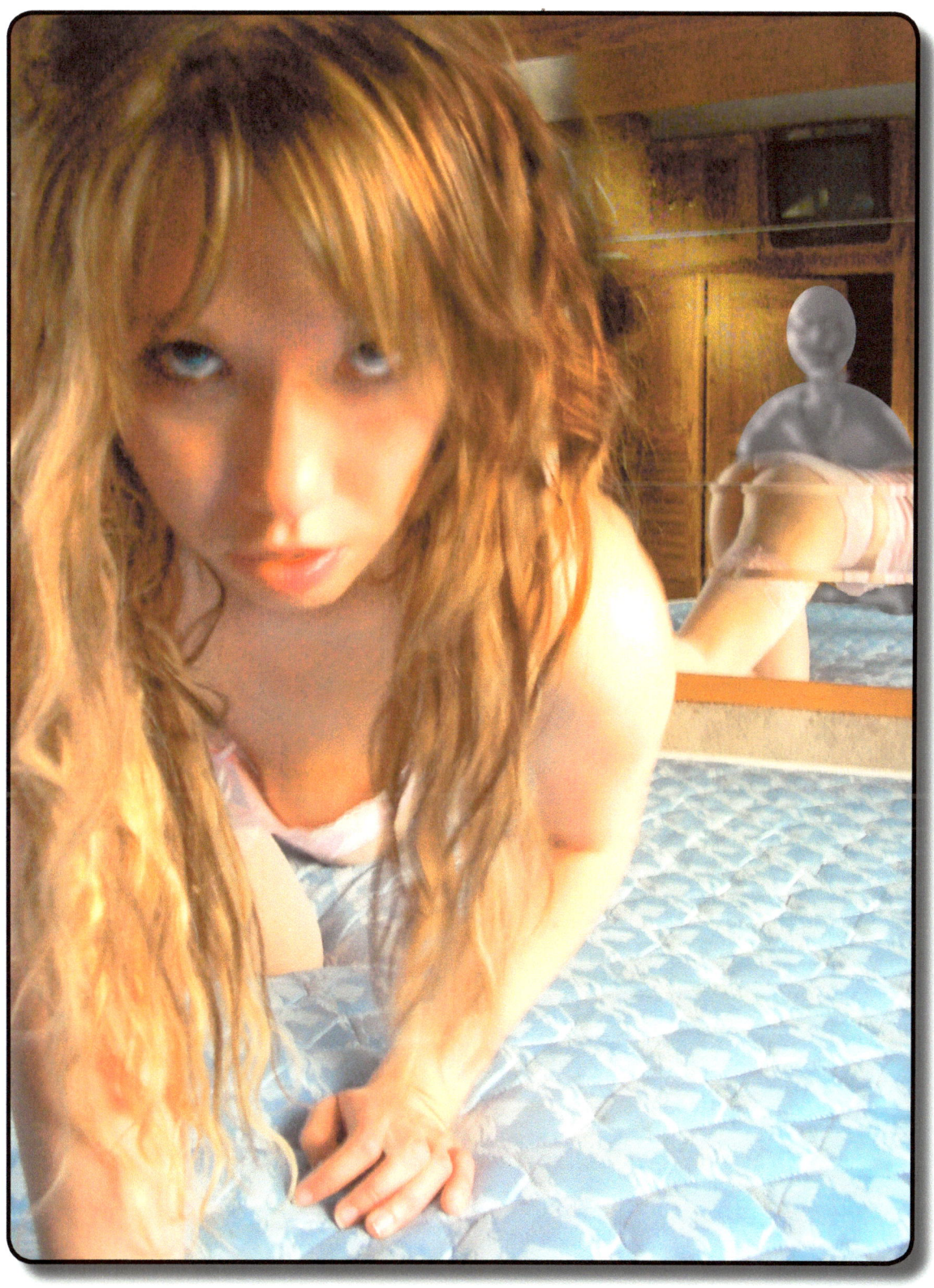

Joyful ghostful

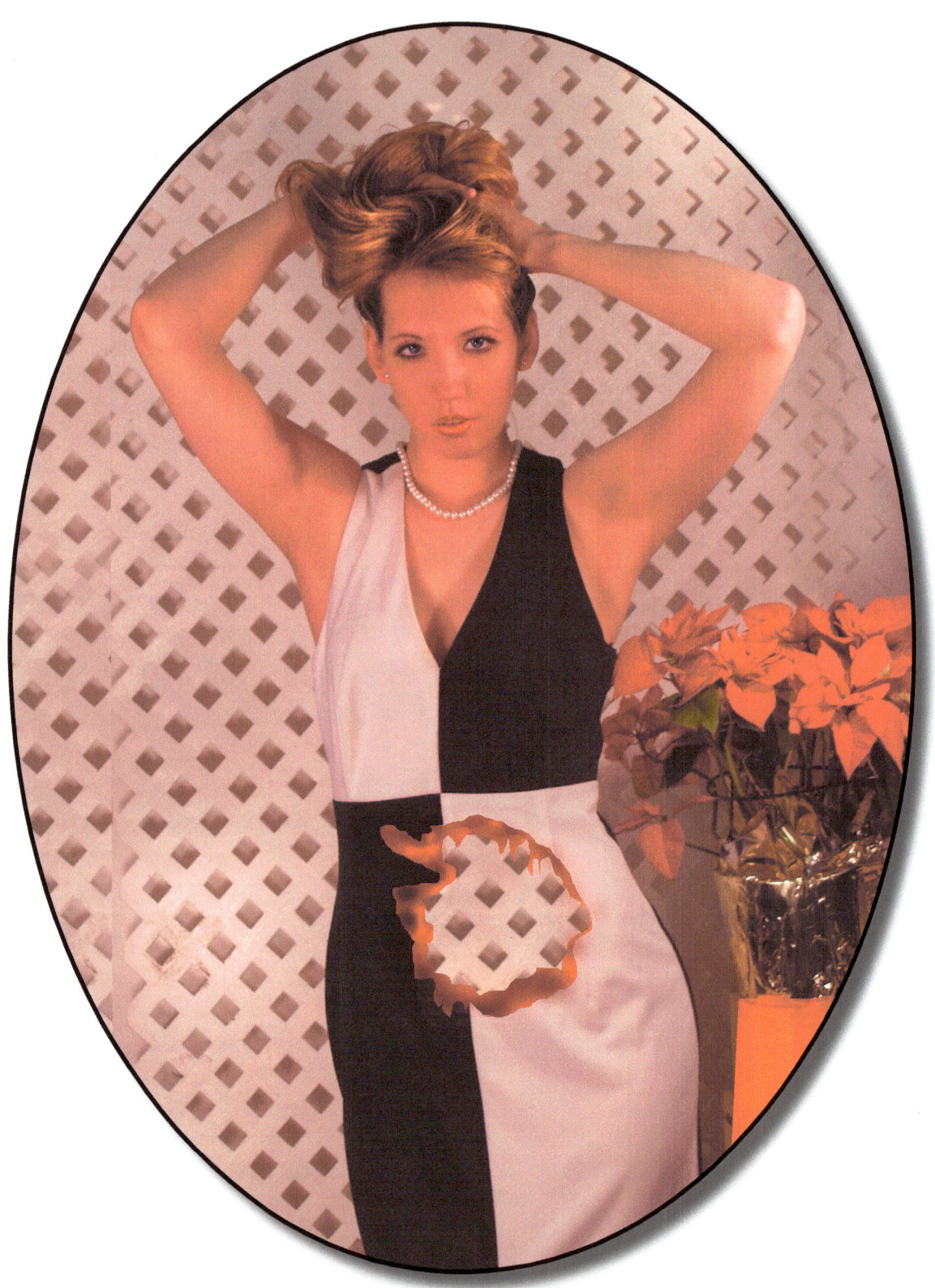

Even on the red carpet, I can see right through you

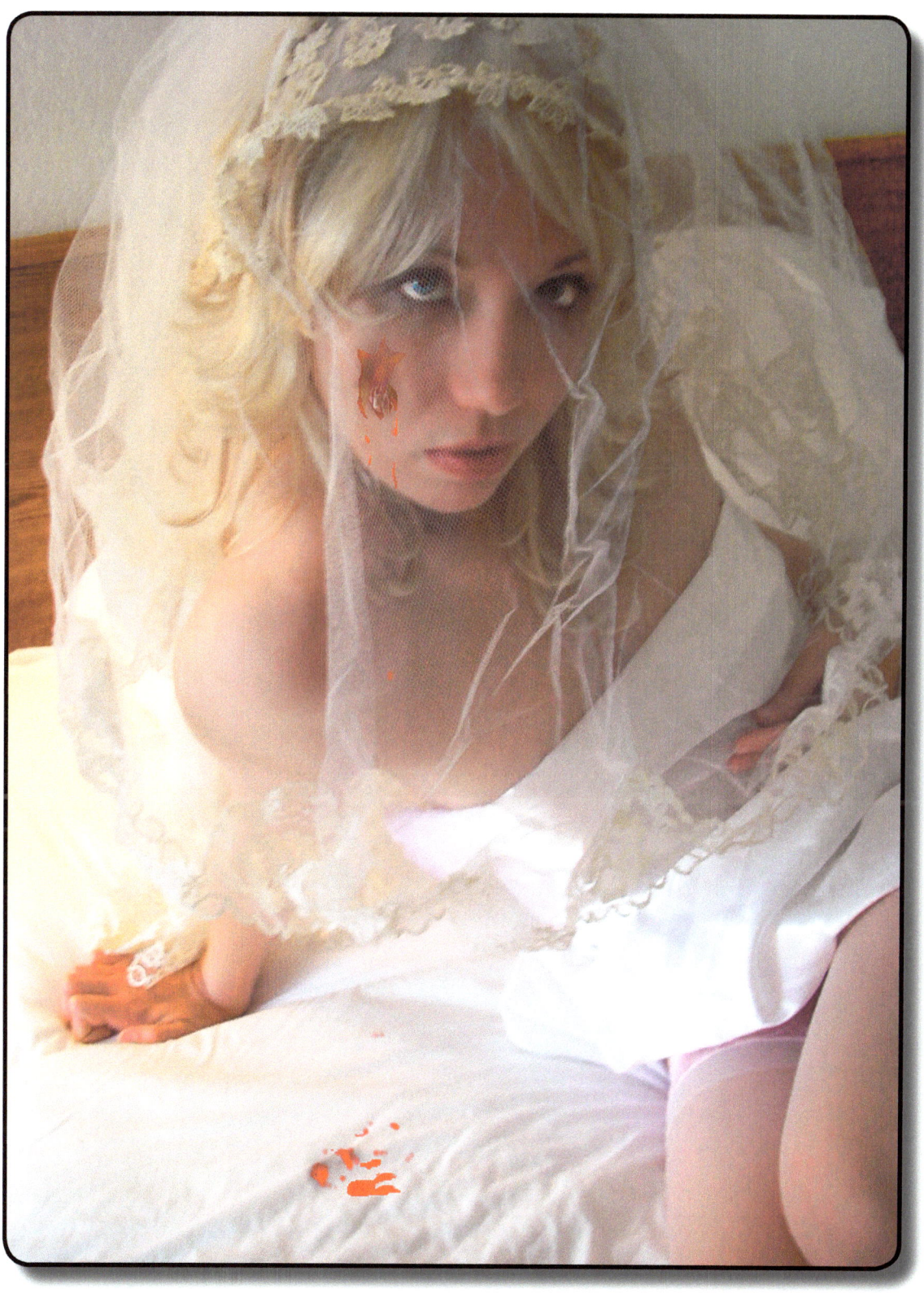

Bad signs from the start

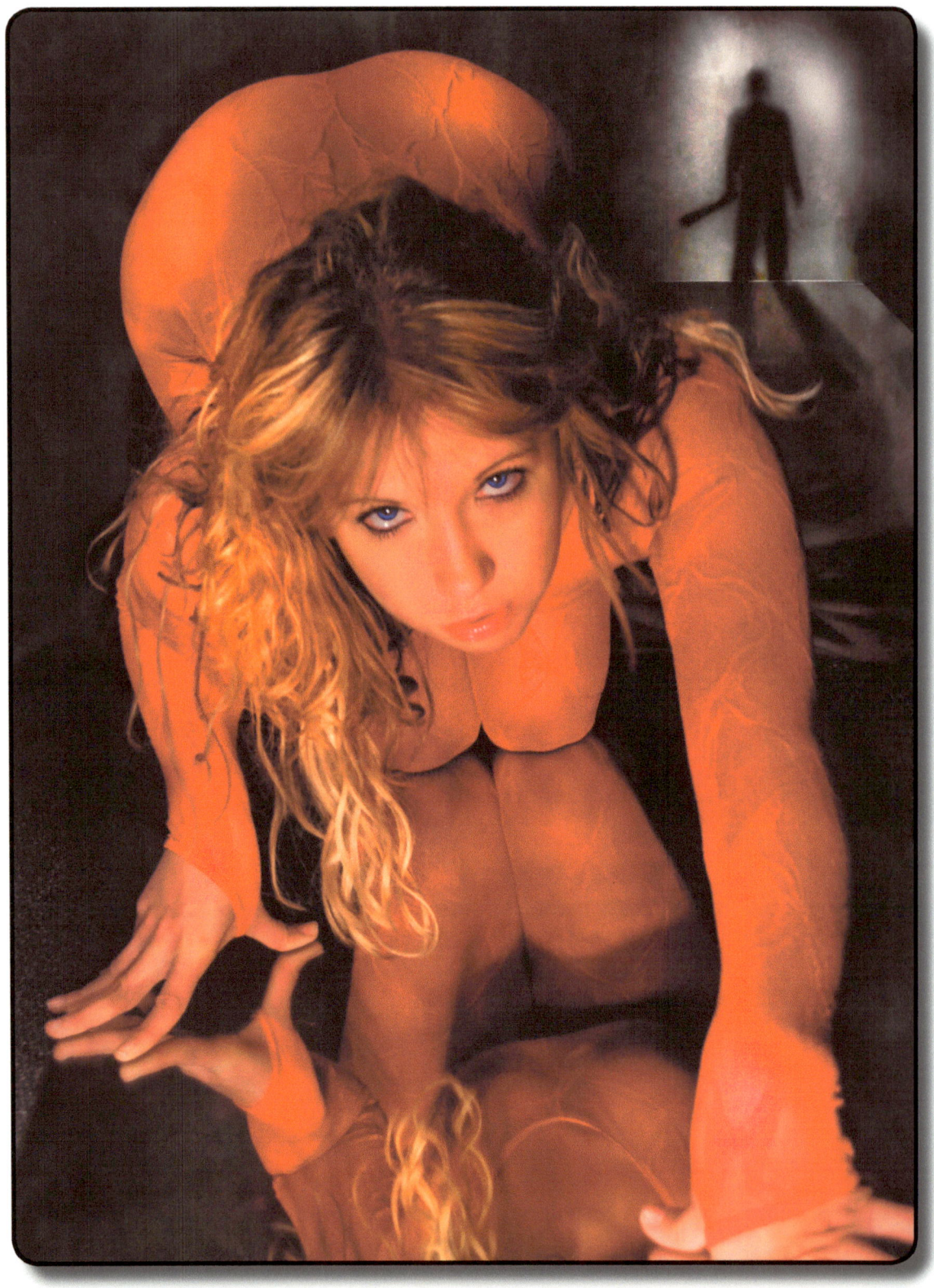

It was a pleasant, joyful night until the other guy decided to show up

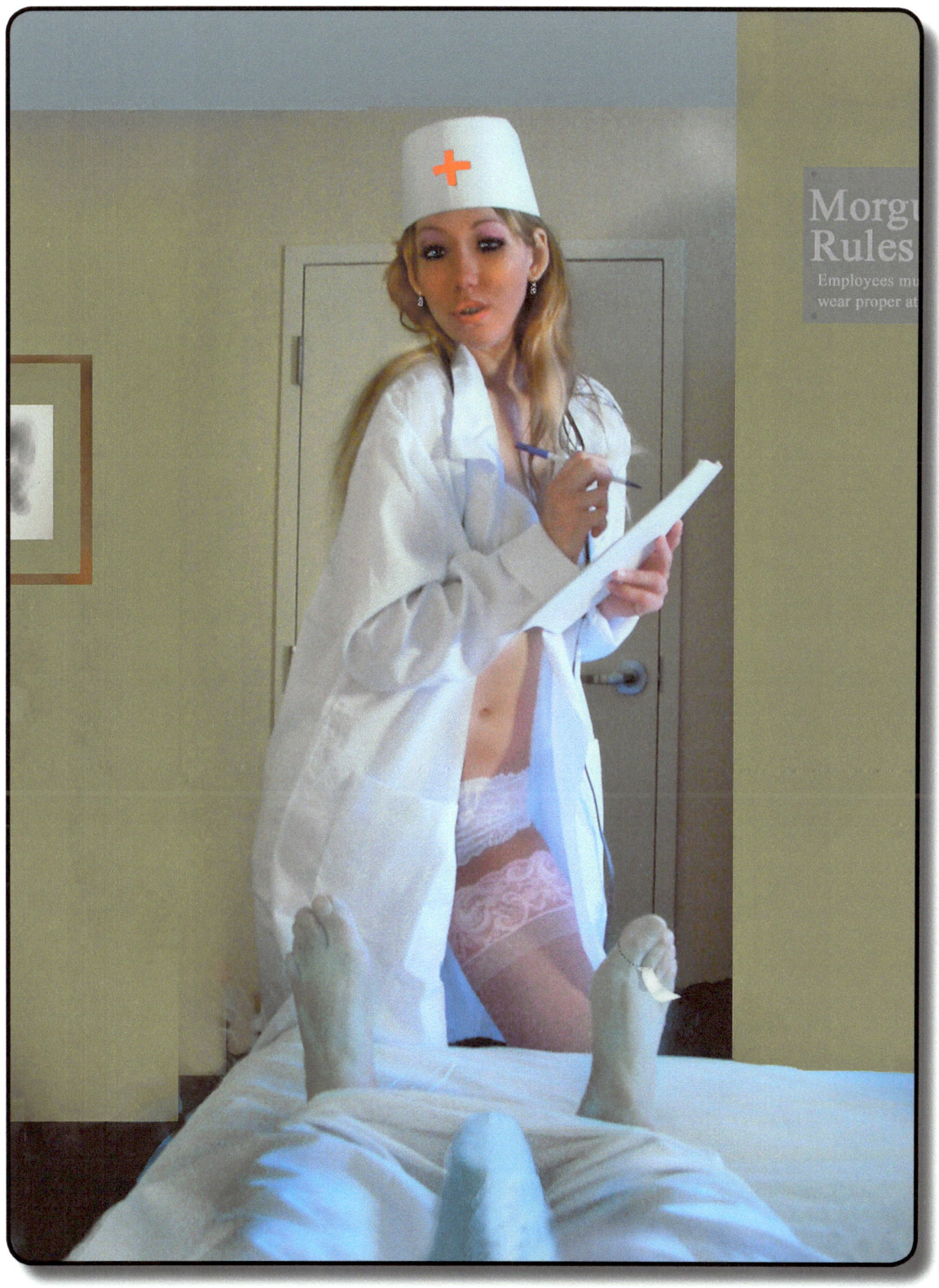

Waking up the dead

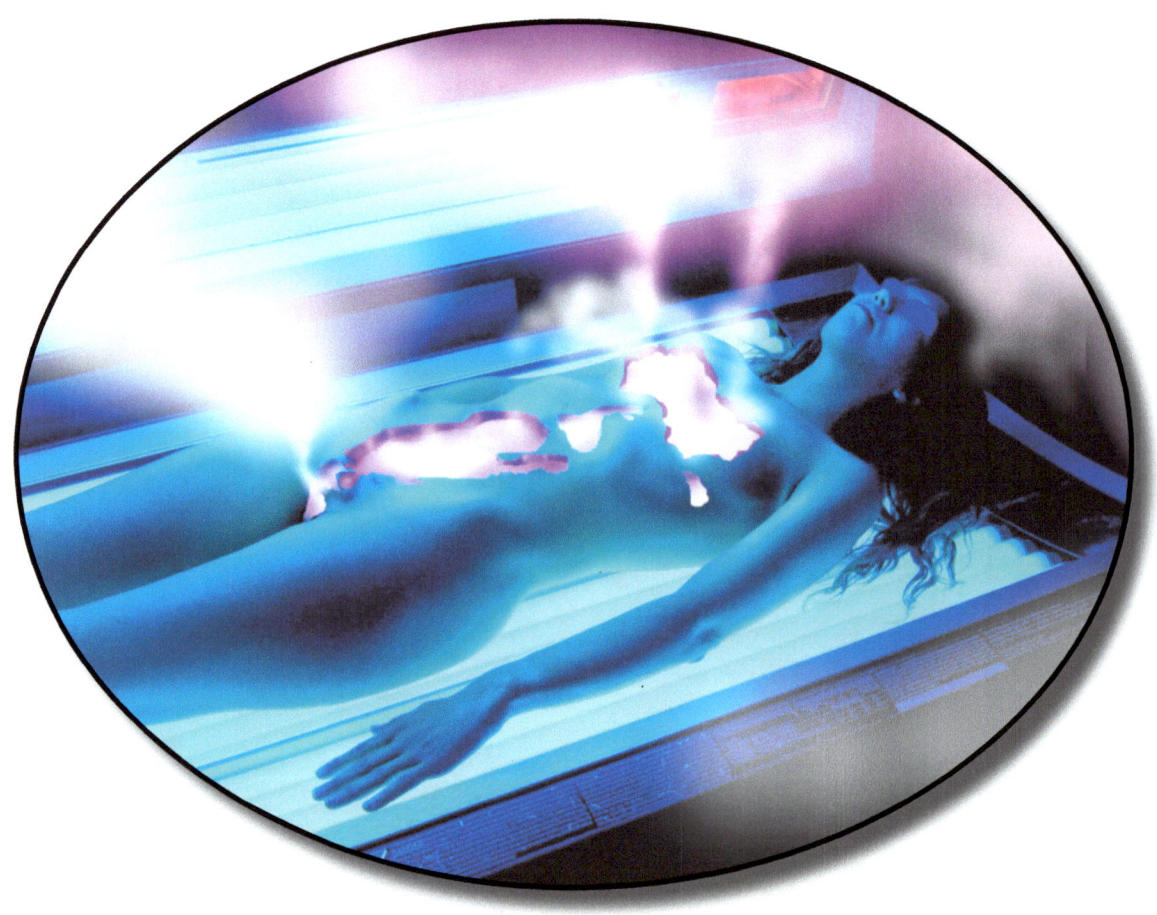

Warning signs of excessive tanning

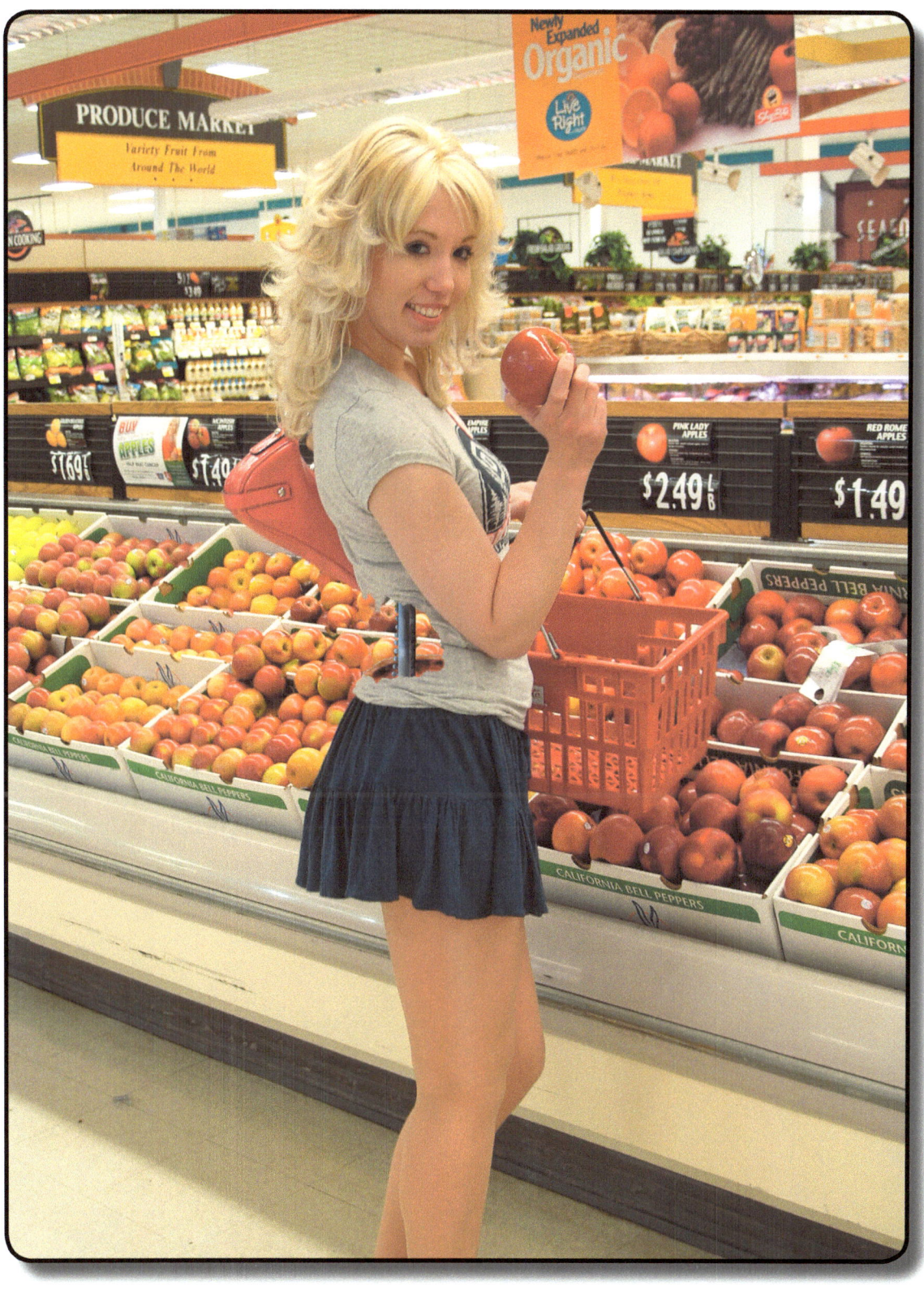

An apple a day keeps the doctor away

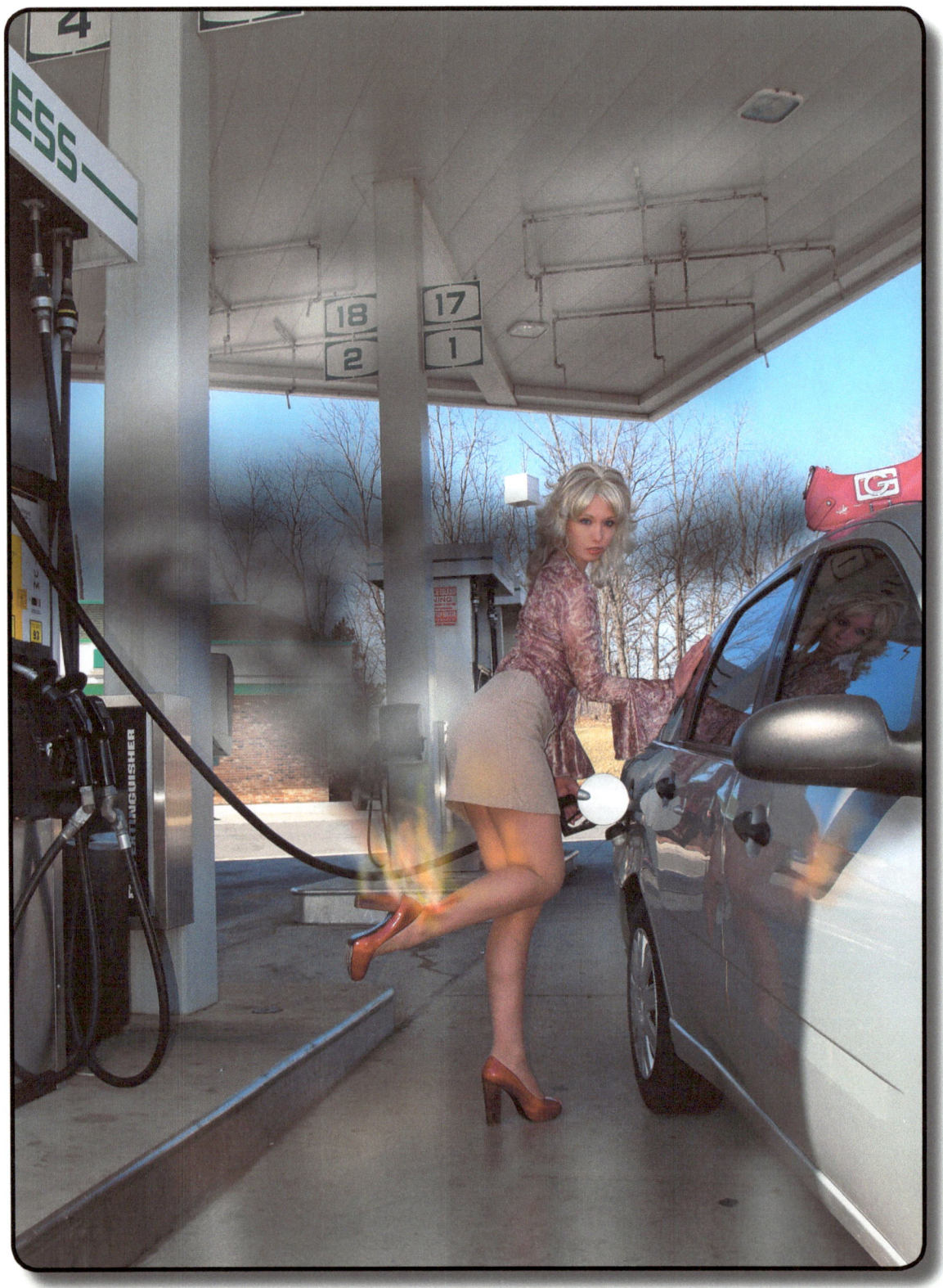

A blonde moment

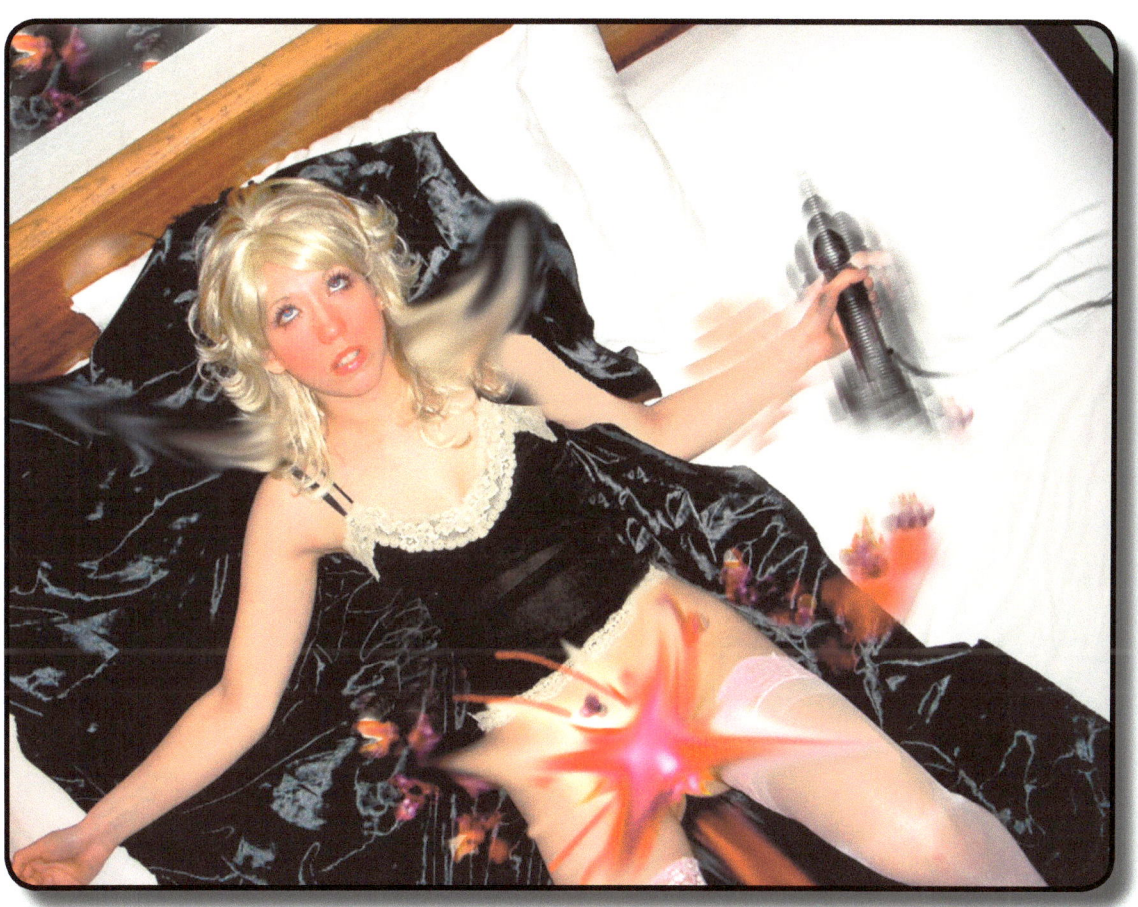

The danger of old fashion plug-in devices

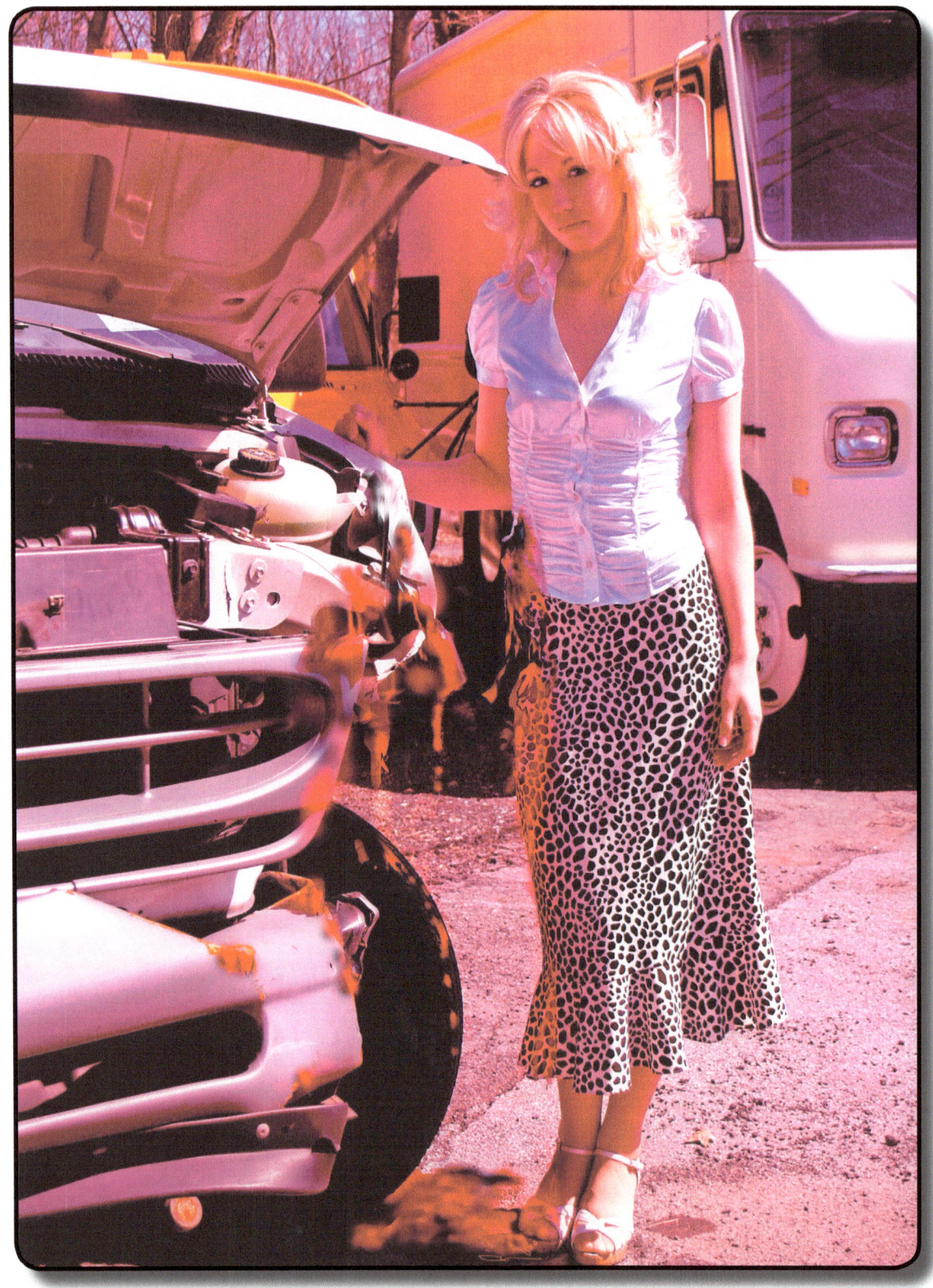

Litigation

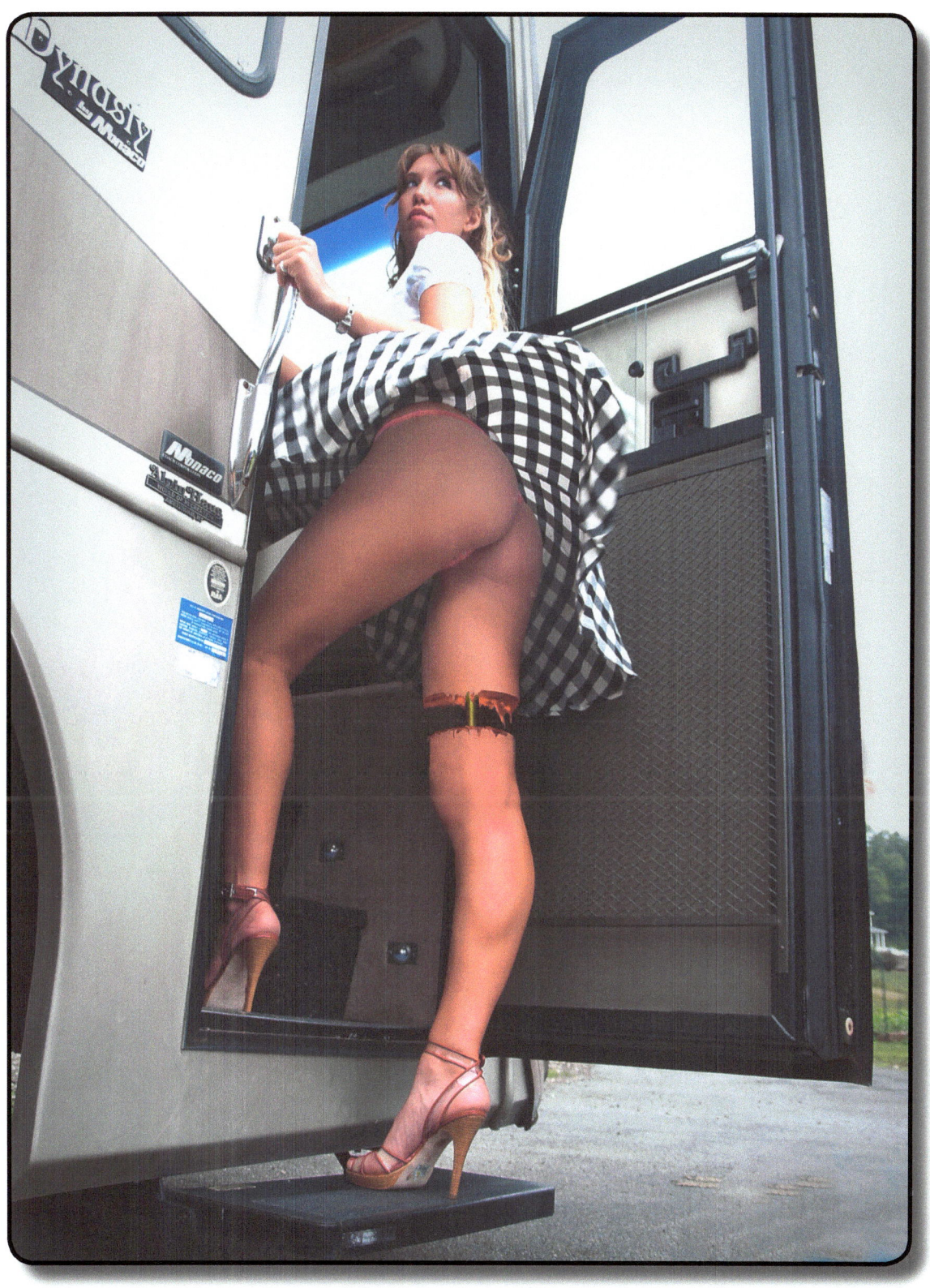

No bad moments with upskirts

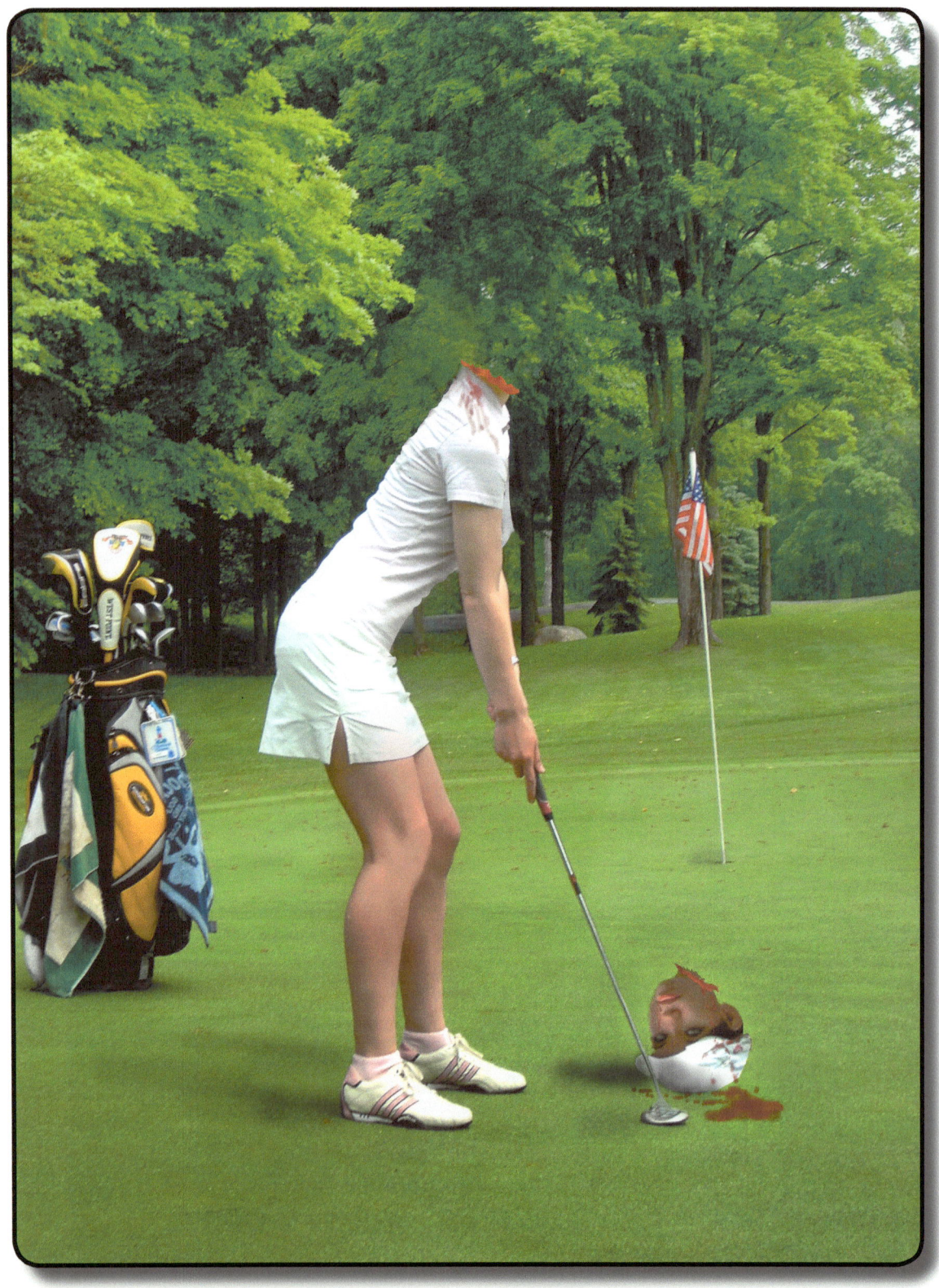

Always use your head if you want to win

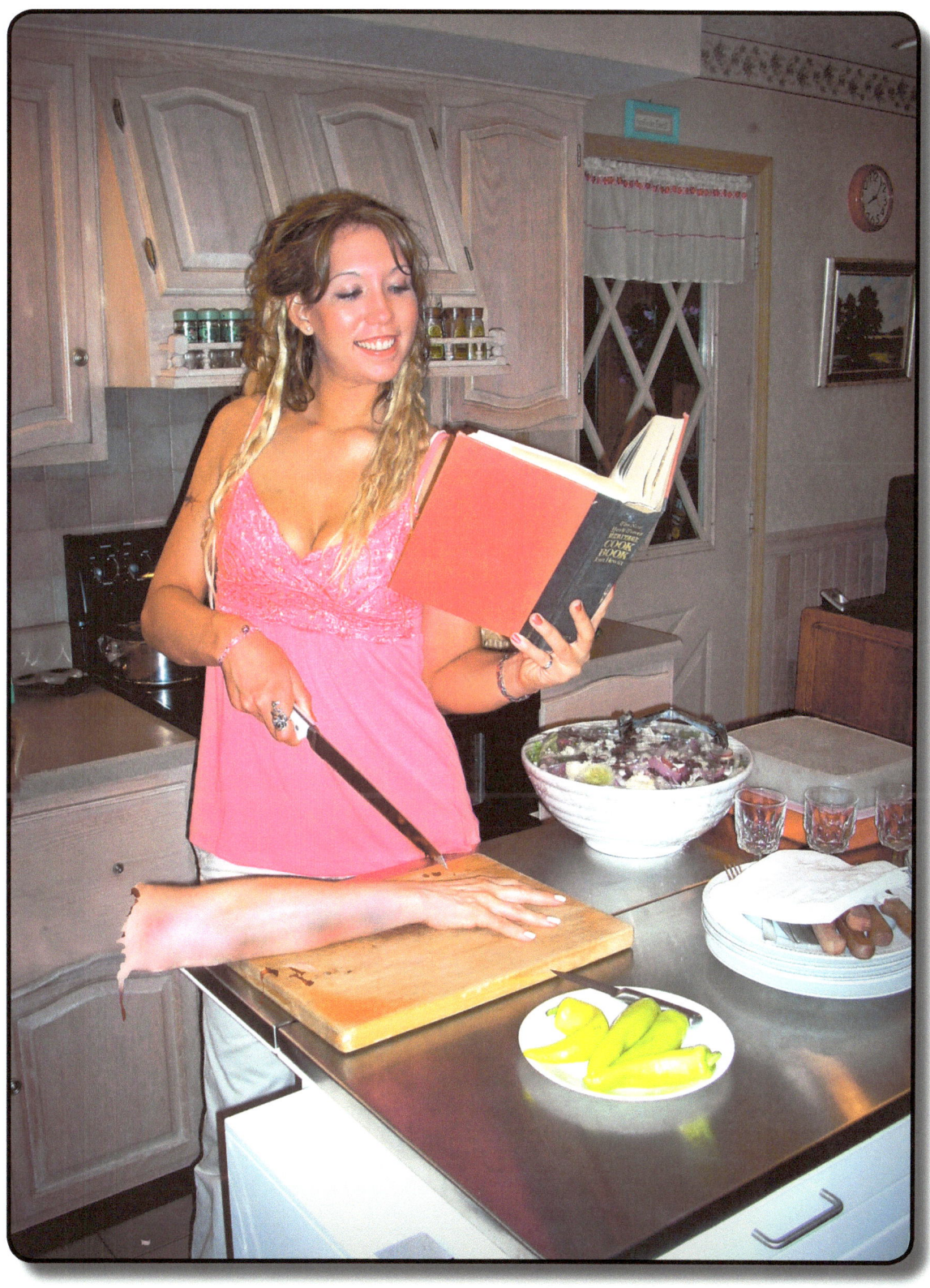

The effect of typos in cook books

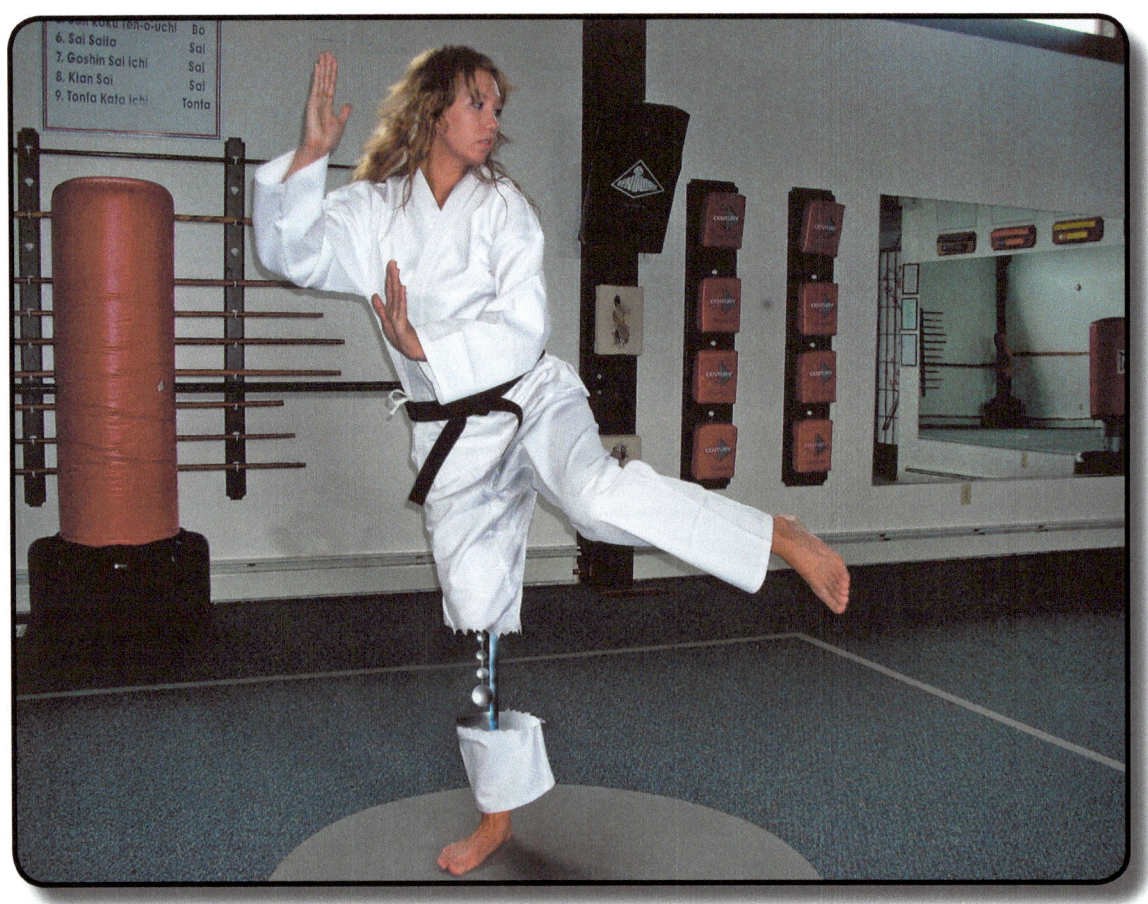

Karate is a mind game anyway

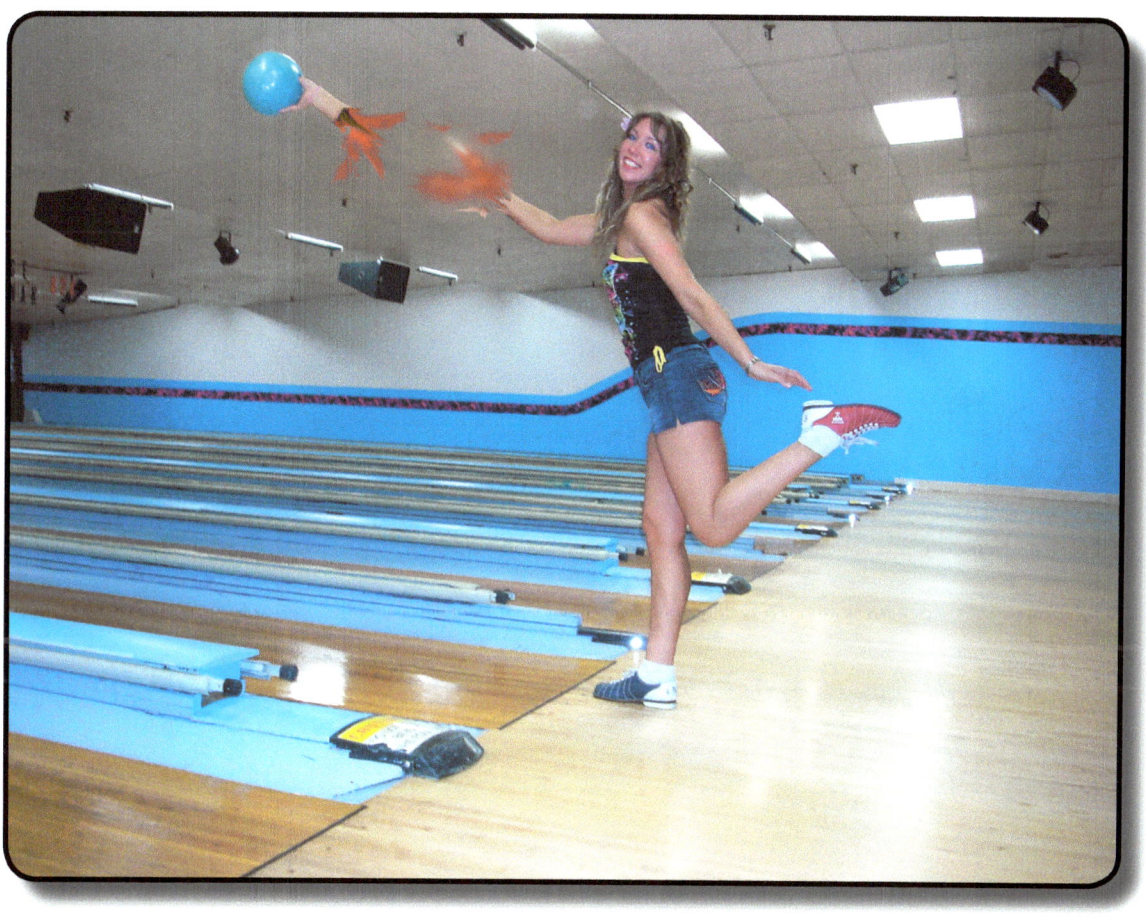

One of your last two strikes

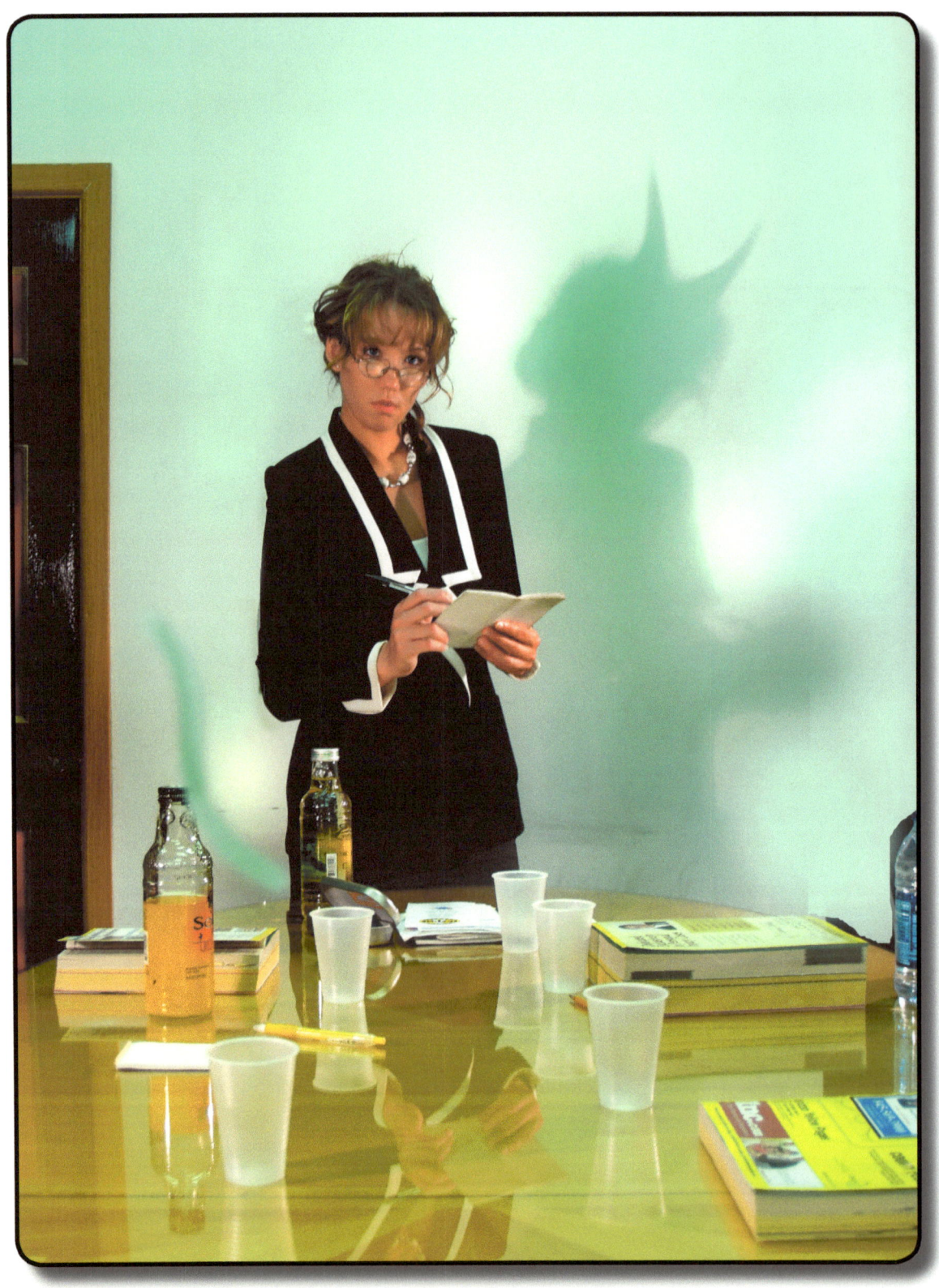

Honesty in corporate meetings is important

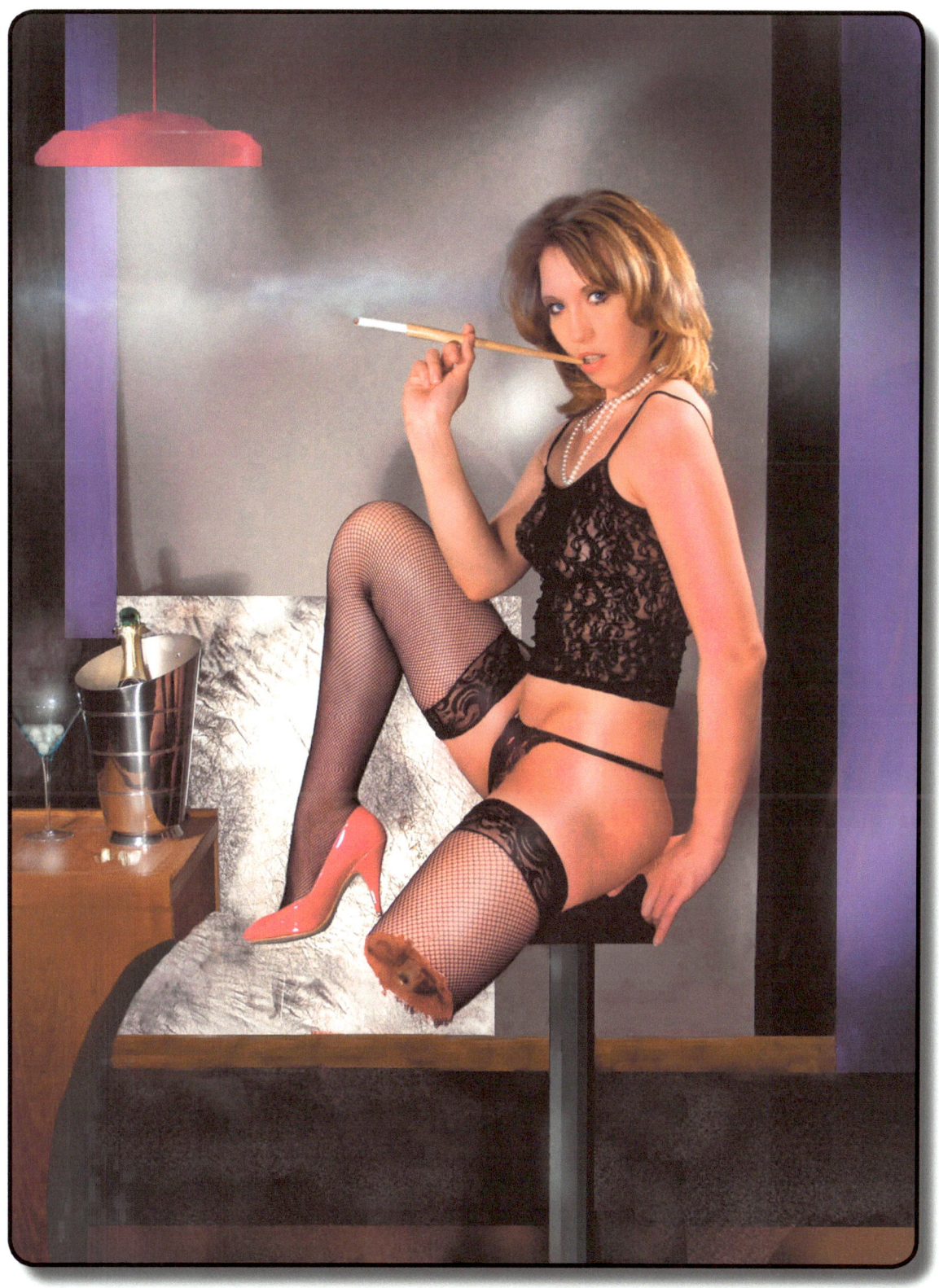

The steady bar patron

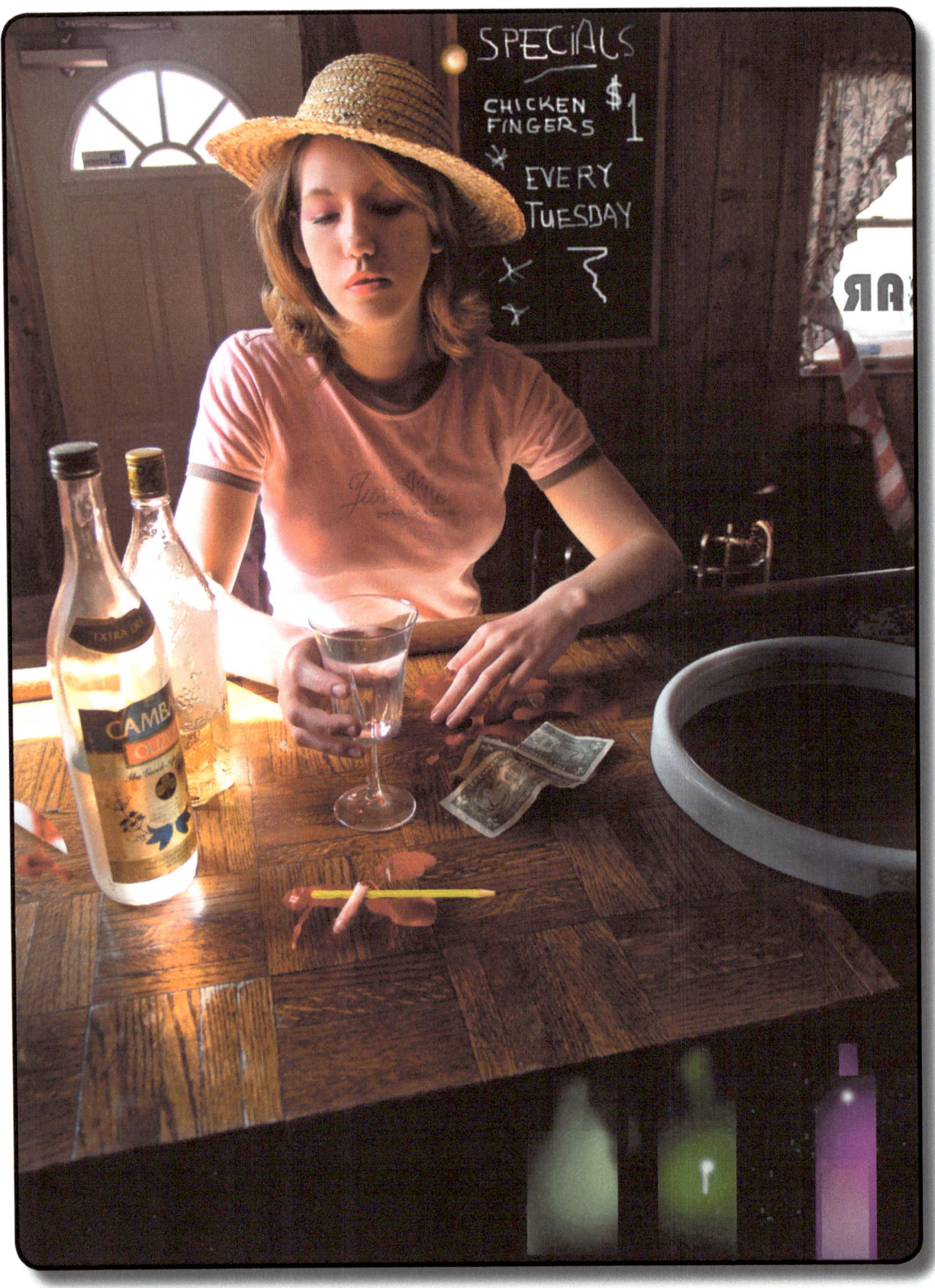

Tuesday at the bar

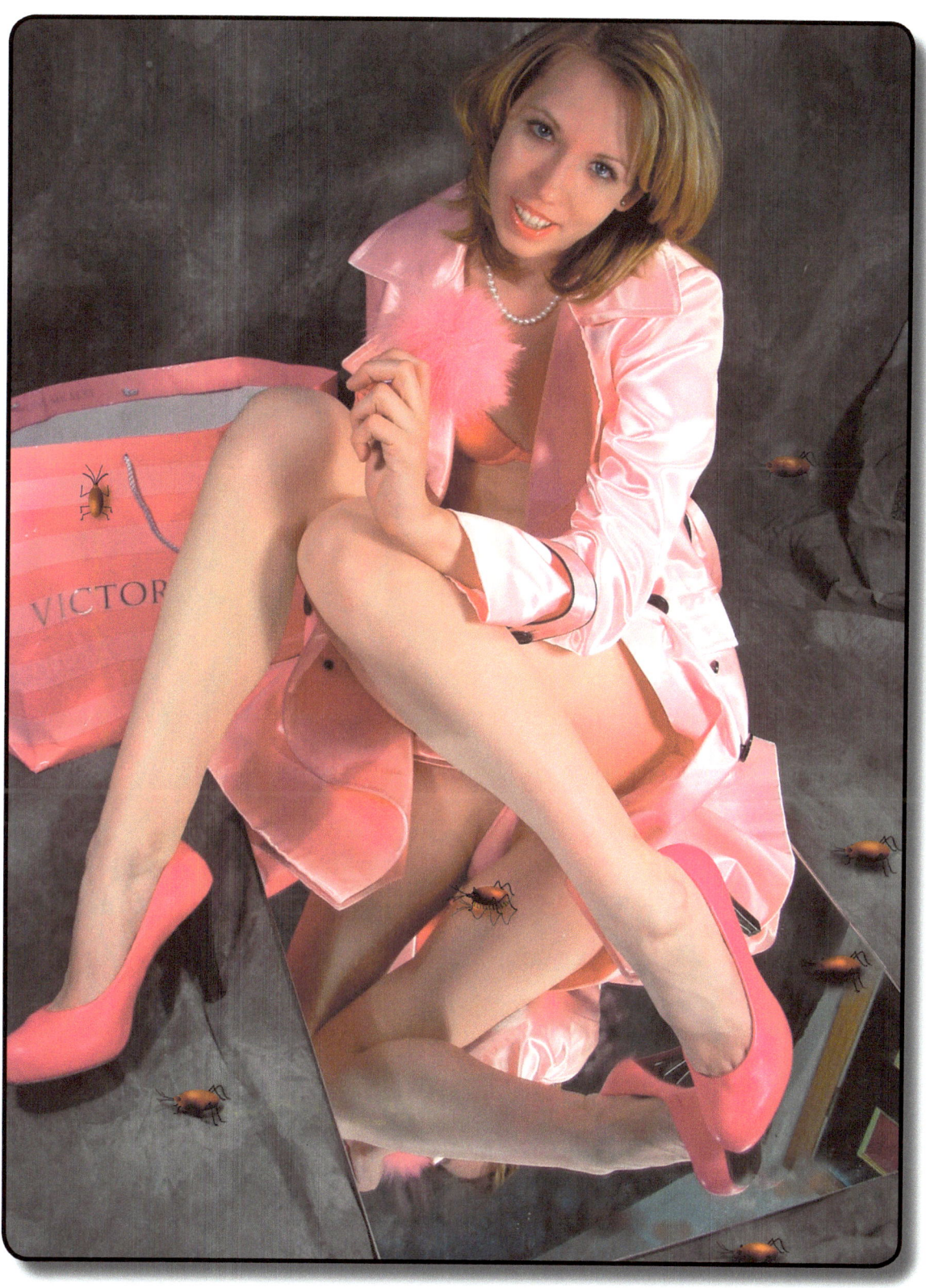

Unwanted secrets

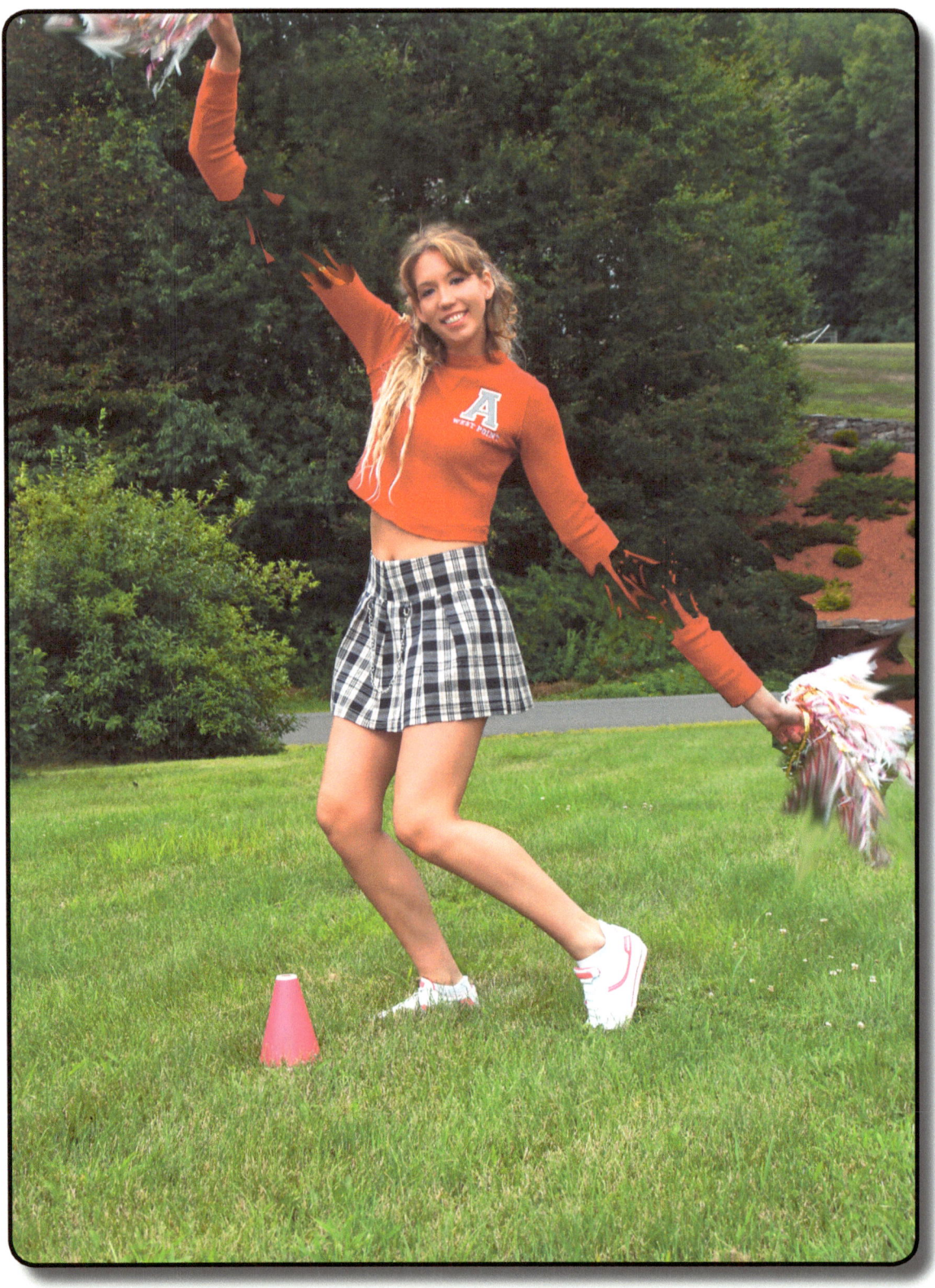

I'll cheer you up...No matter what

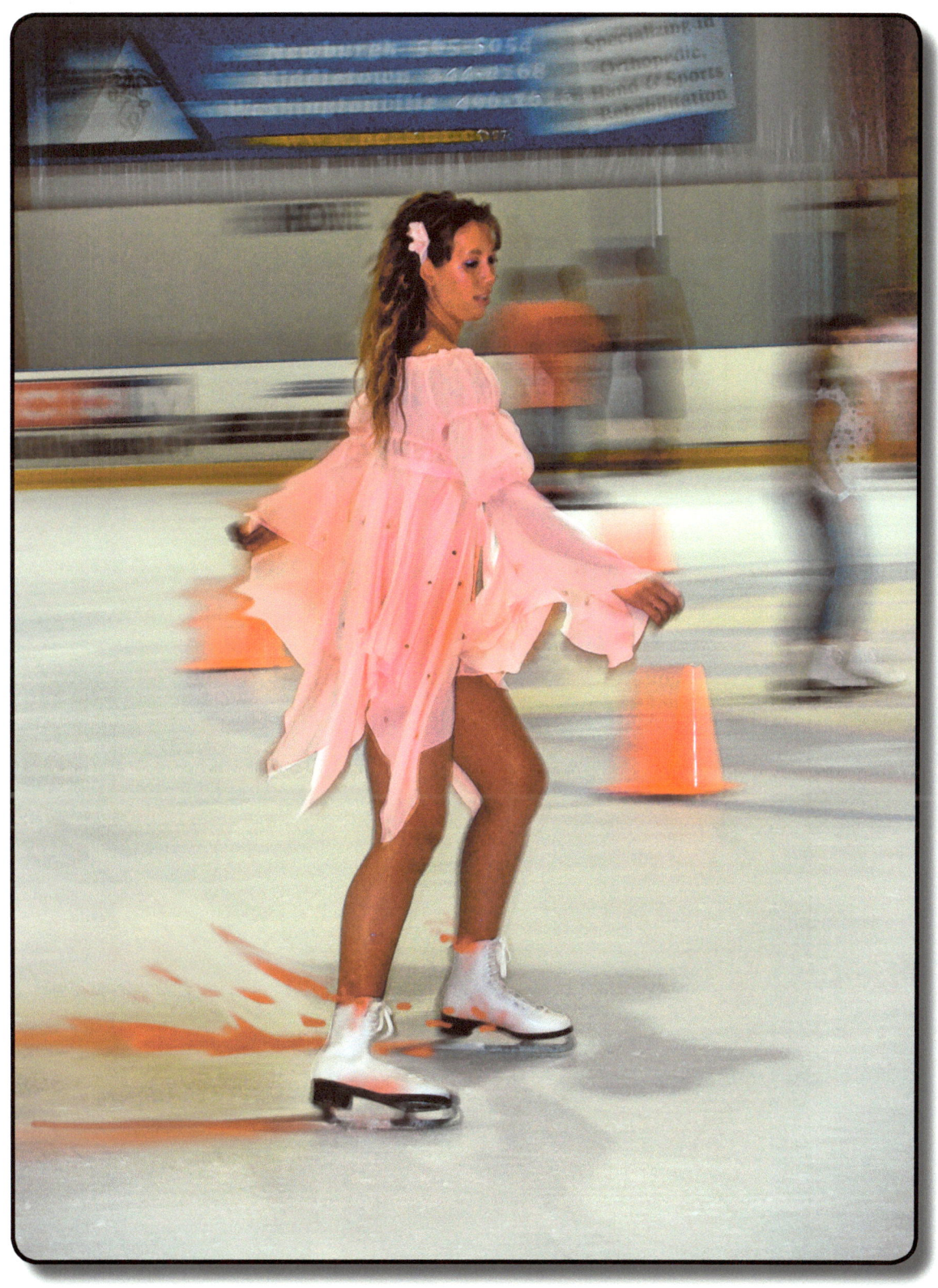

Never give up the fun

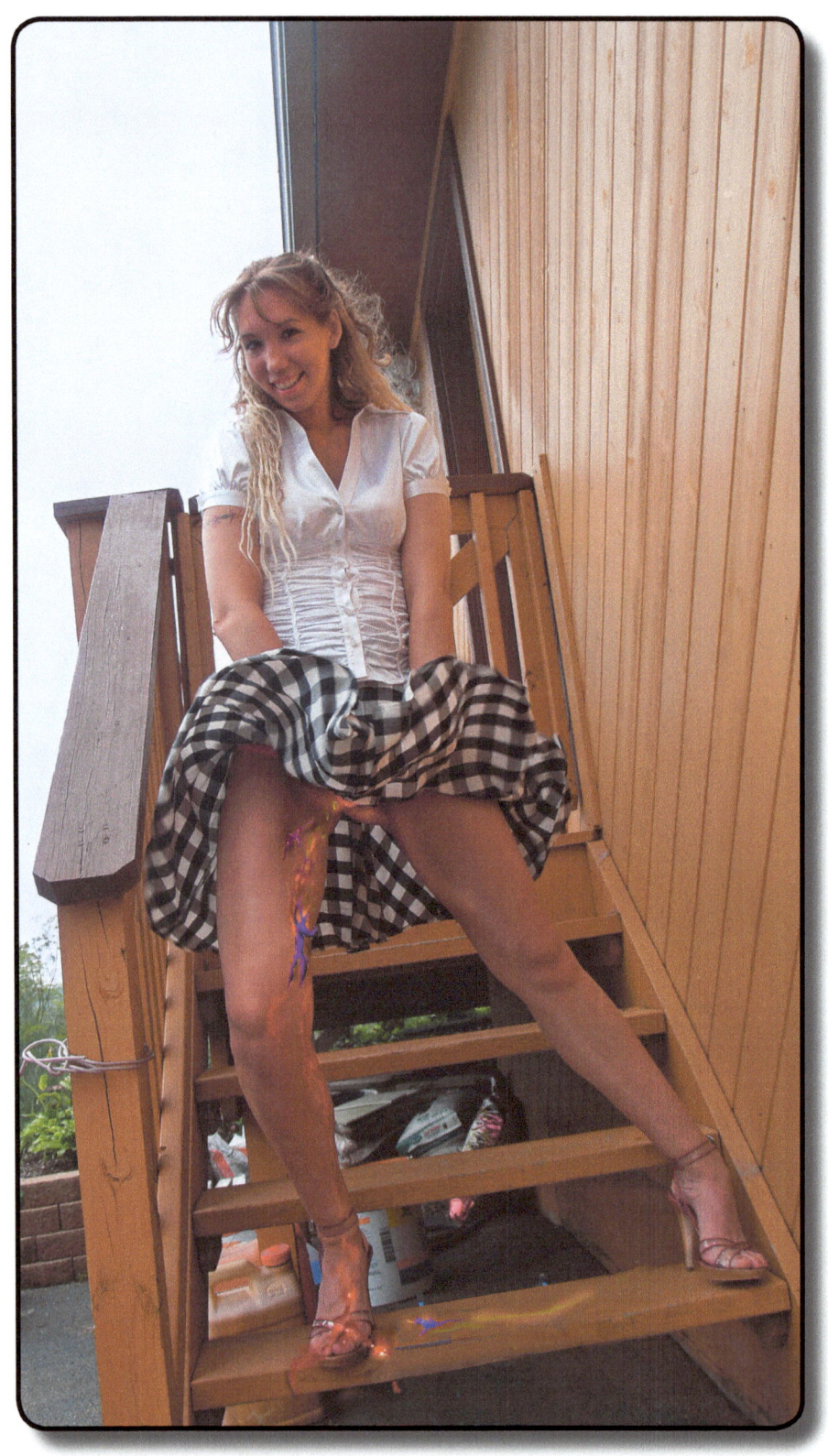

Regardless of race or color, we are all climbing upwards

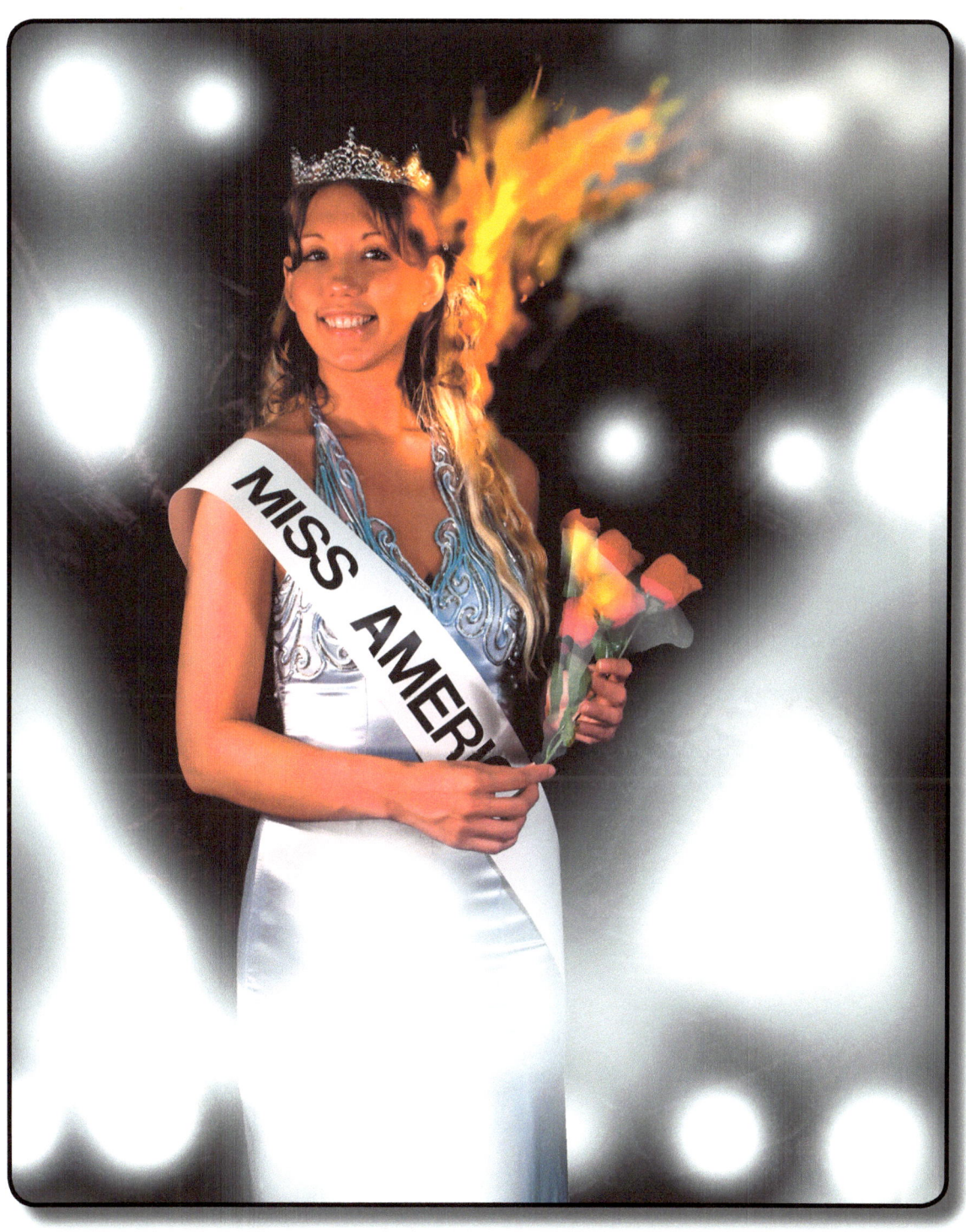

On top

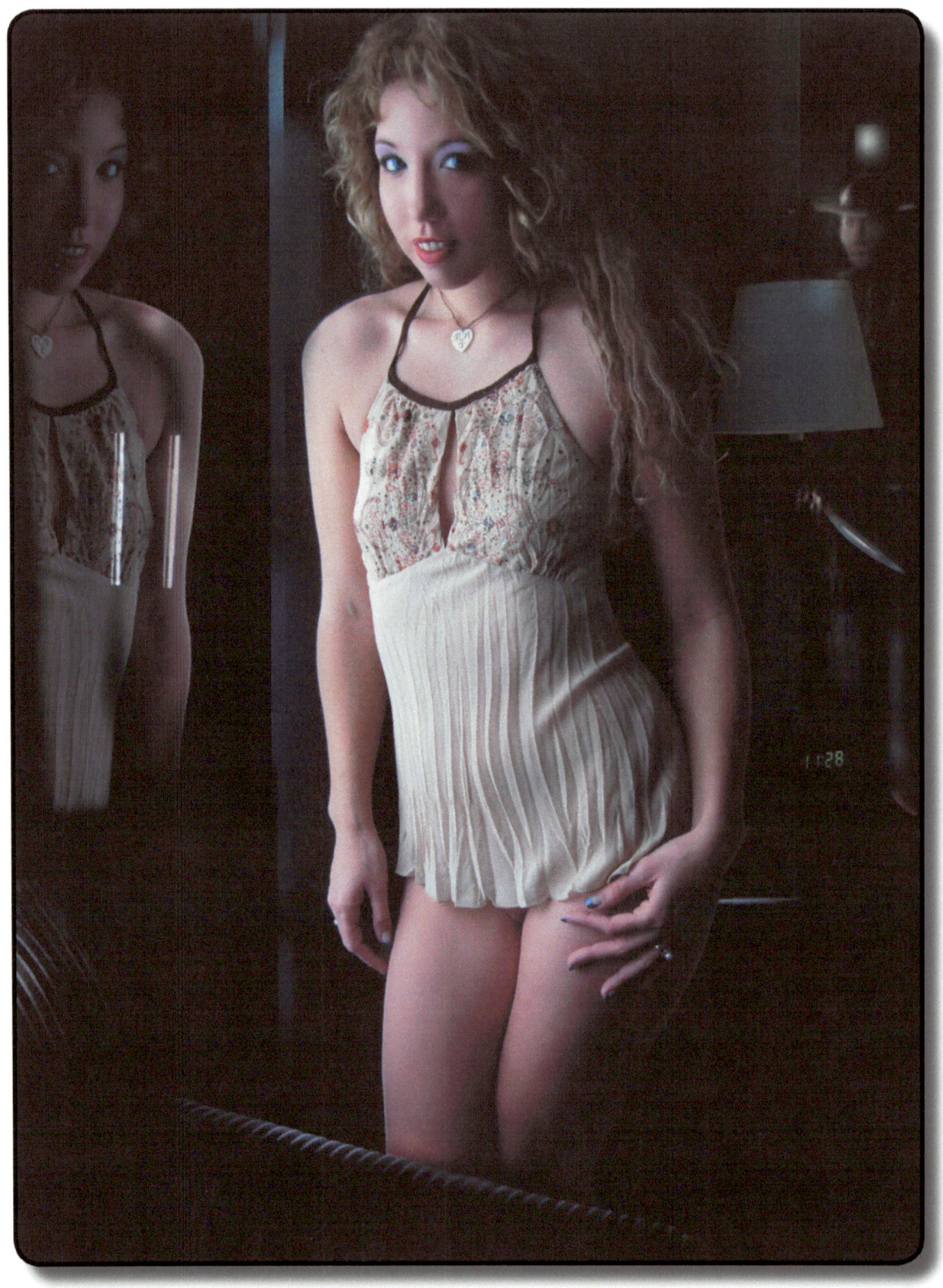

I see you in the mirror.... Is that you Bob?

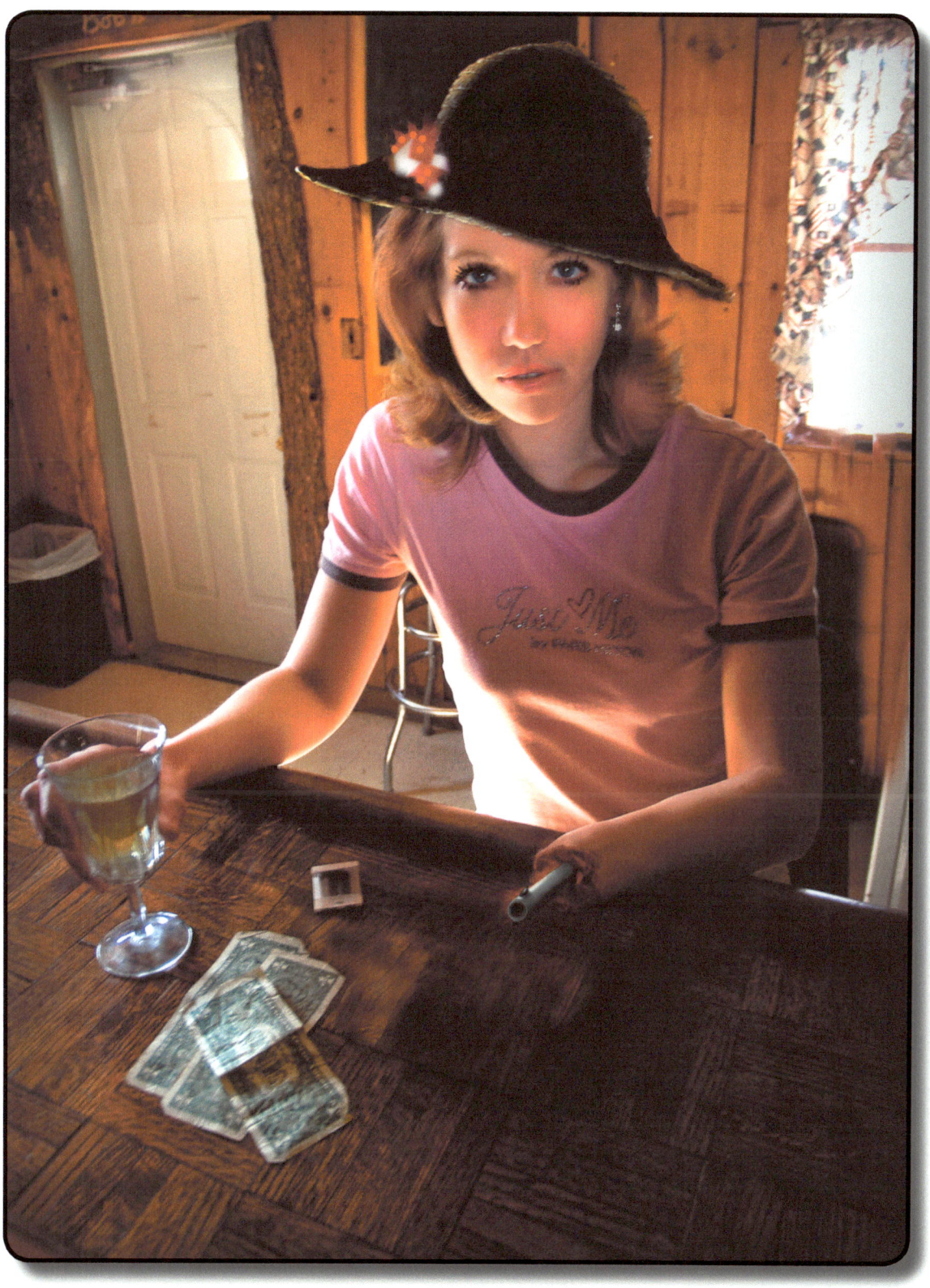

Hand over the money!

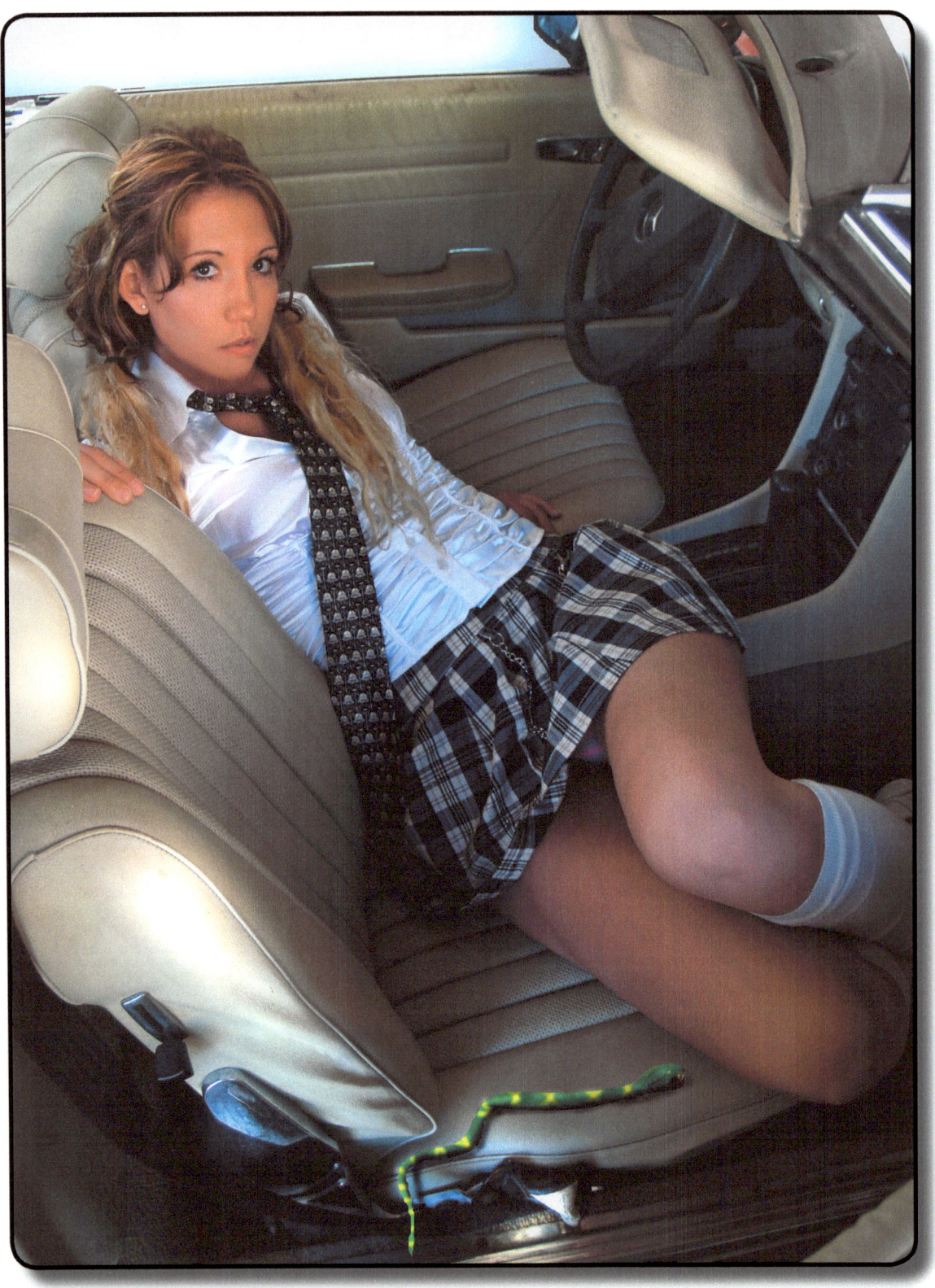

Hidden treasures of luxury cars are unforgettable

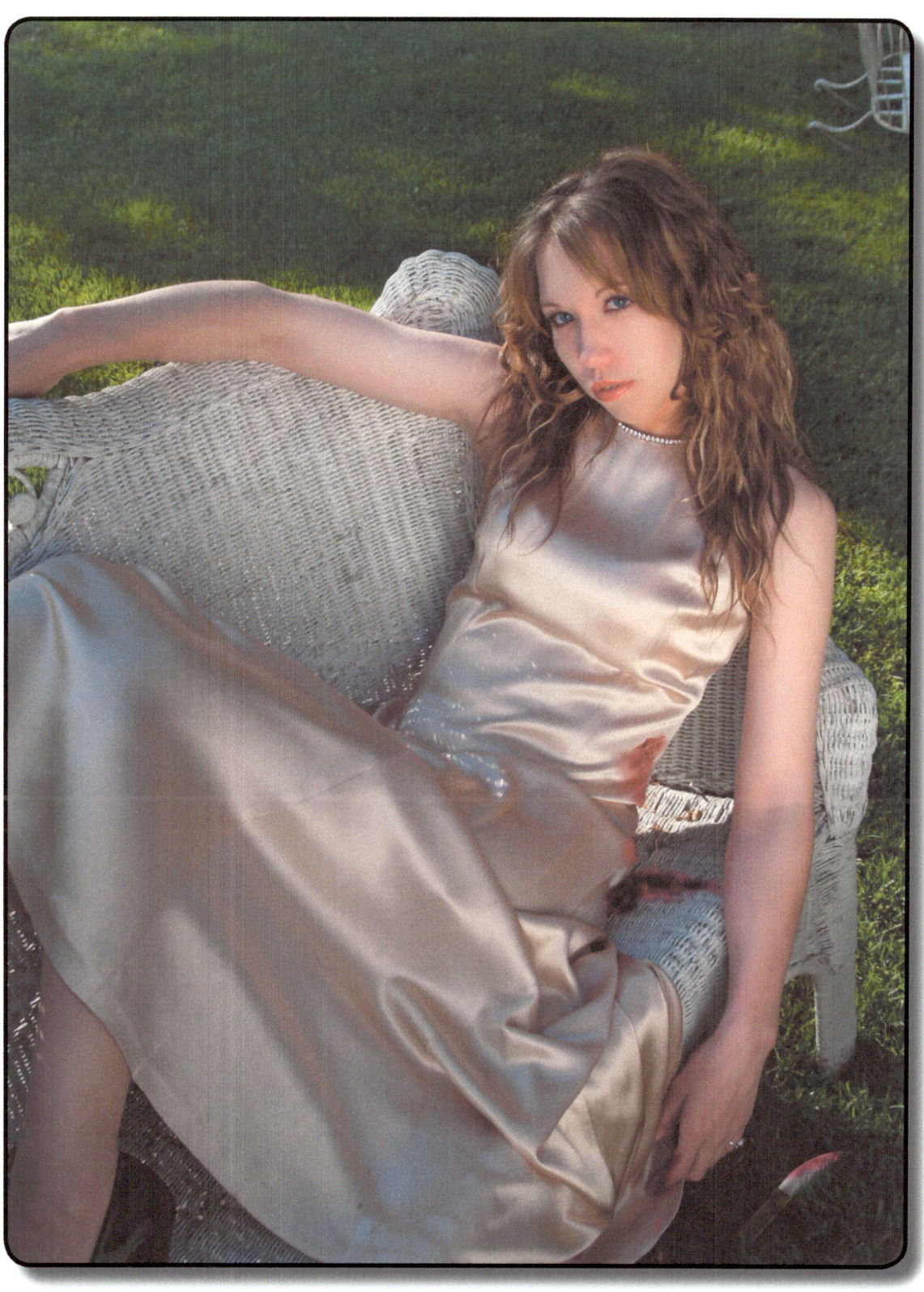

The unbearable pressure of being beauty sometimes takes its toll

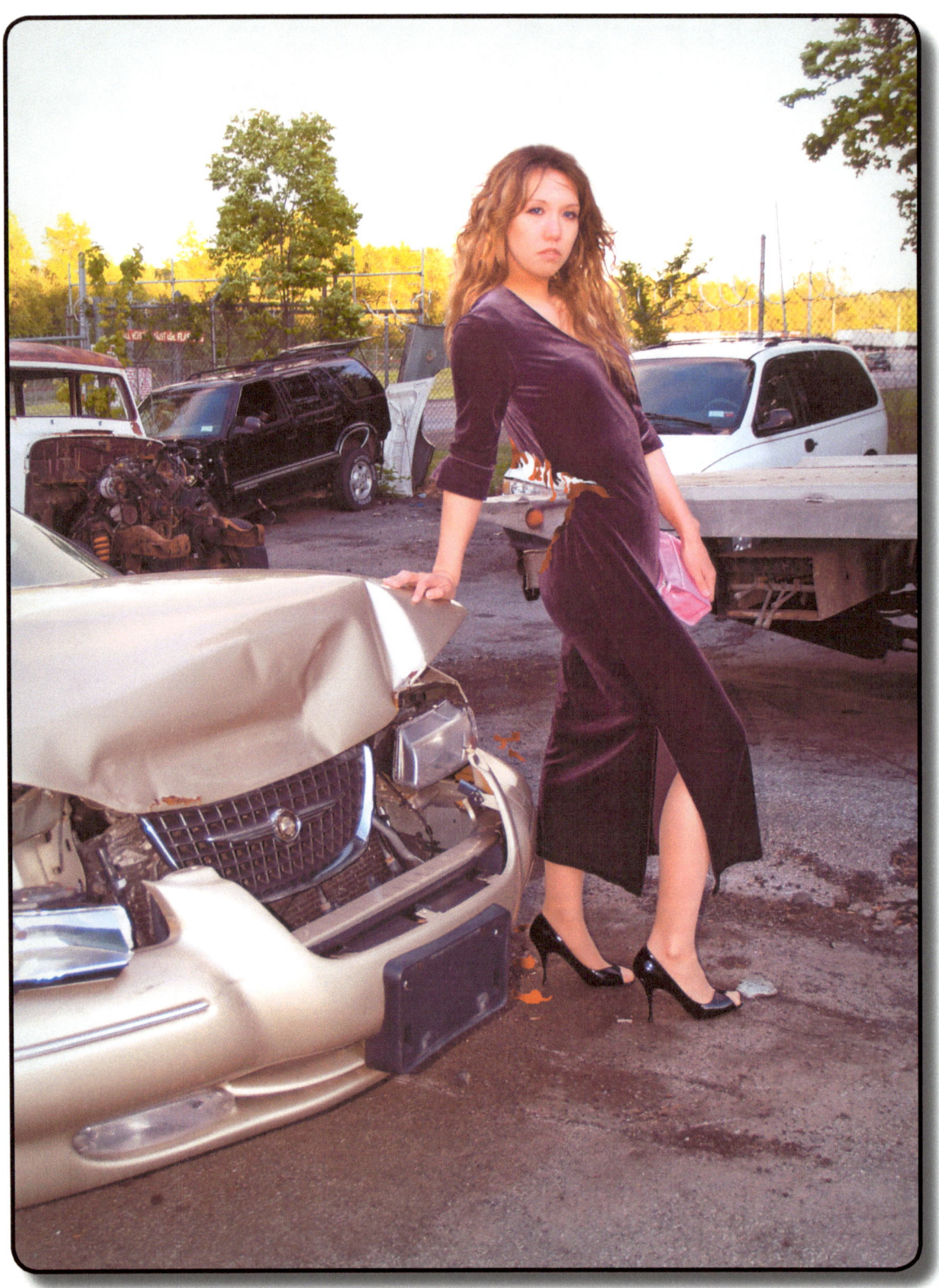

The glamour of junk yard

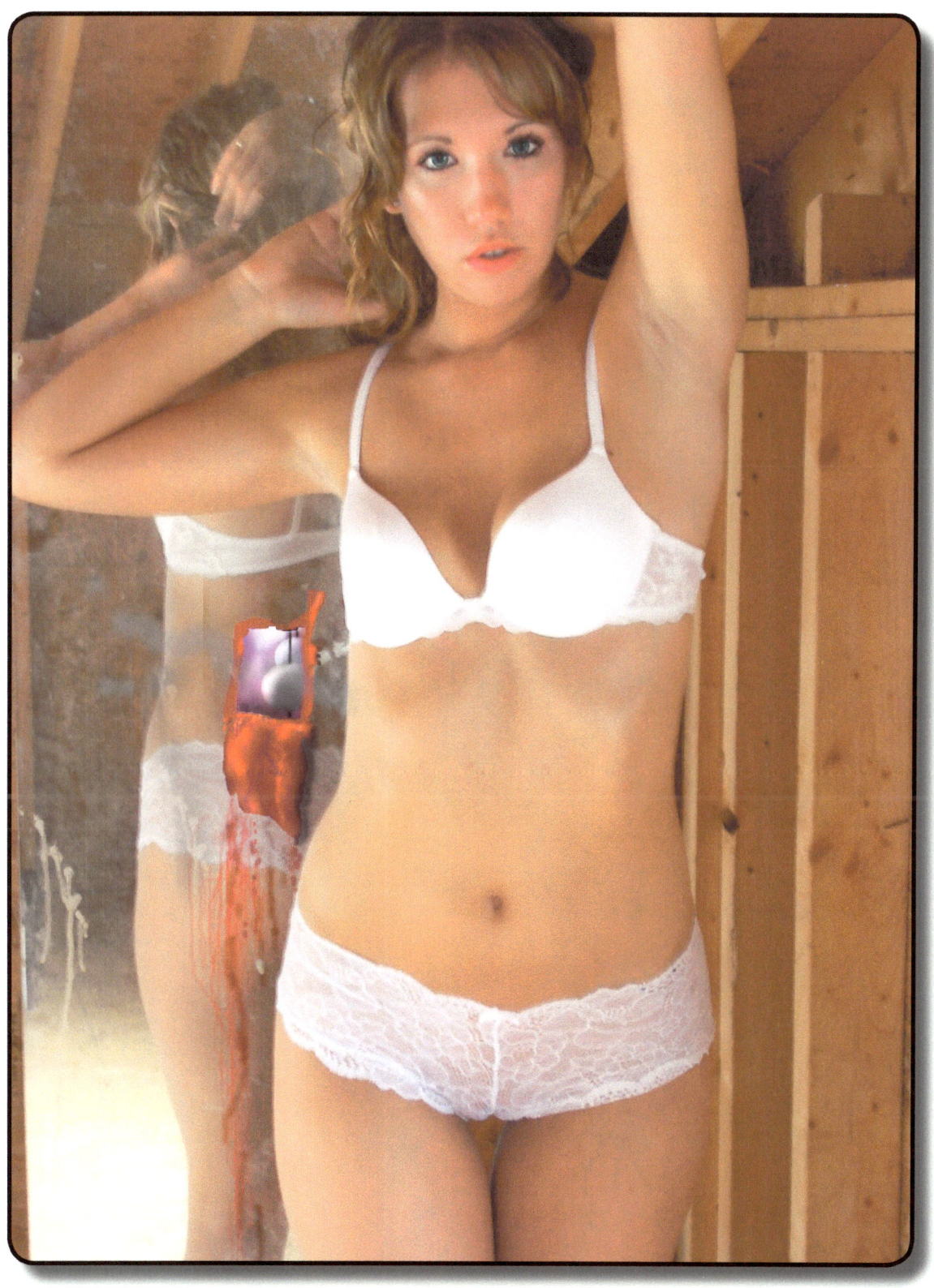

Mirrors always show some imperfections

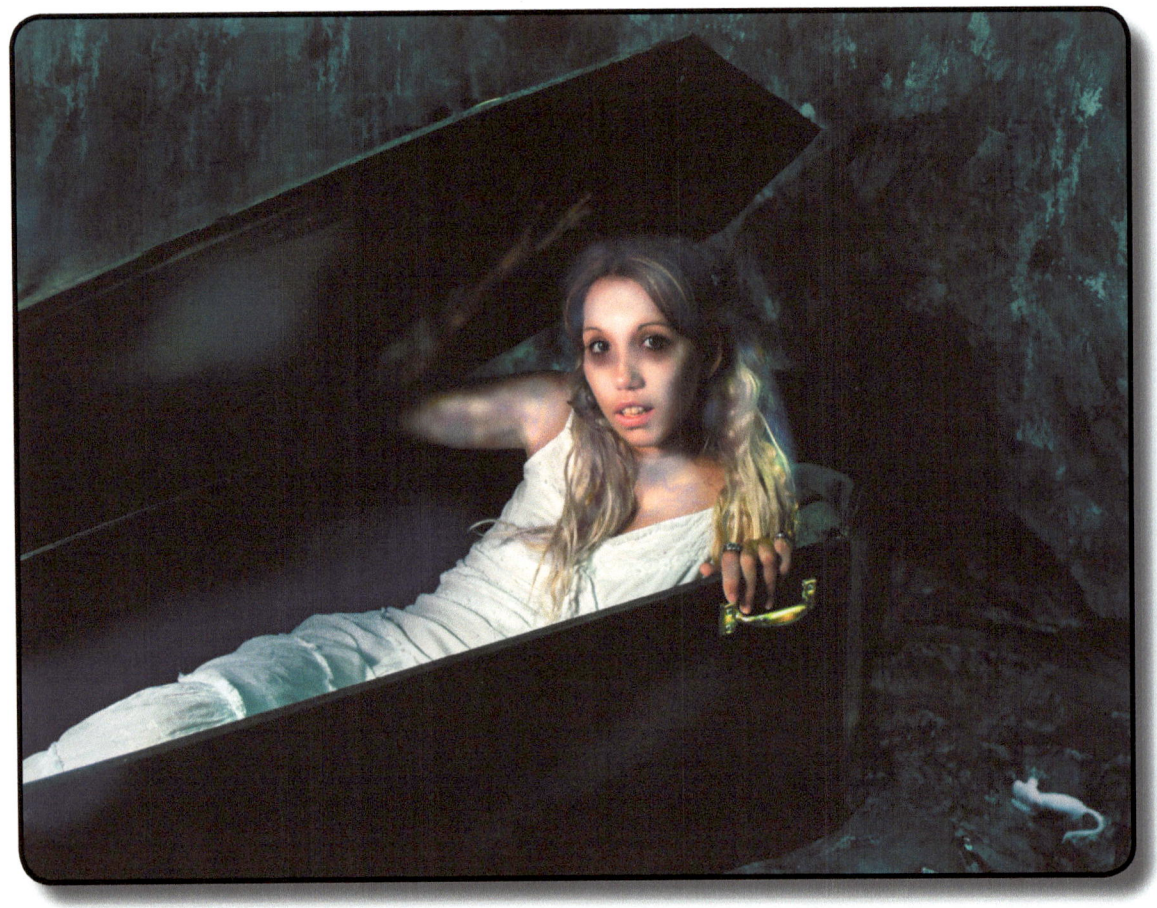

I'd rather die then come out from this coffin and face the sleeping mouse

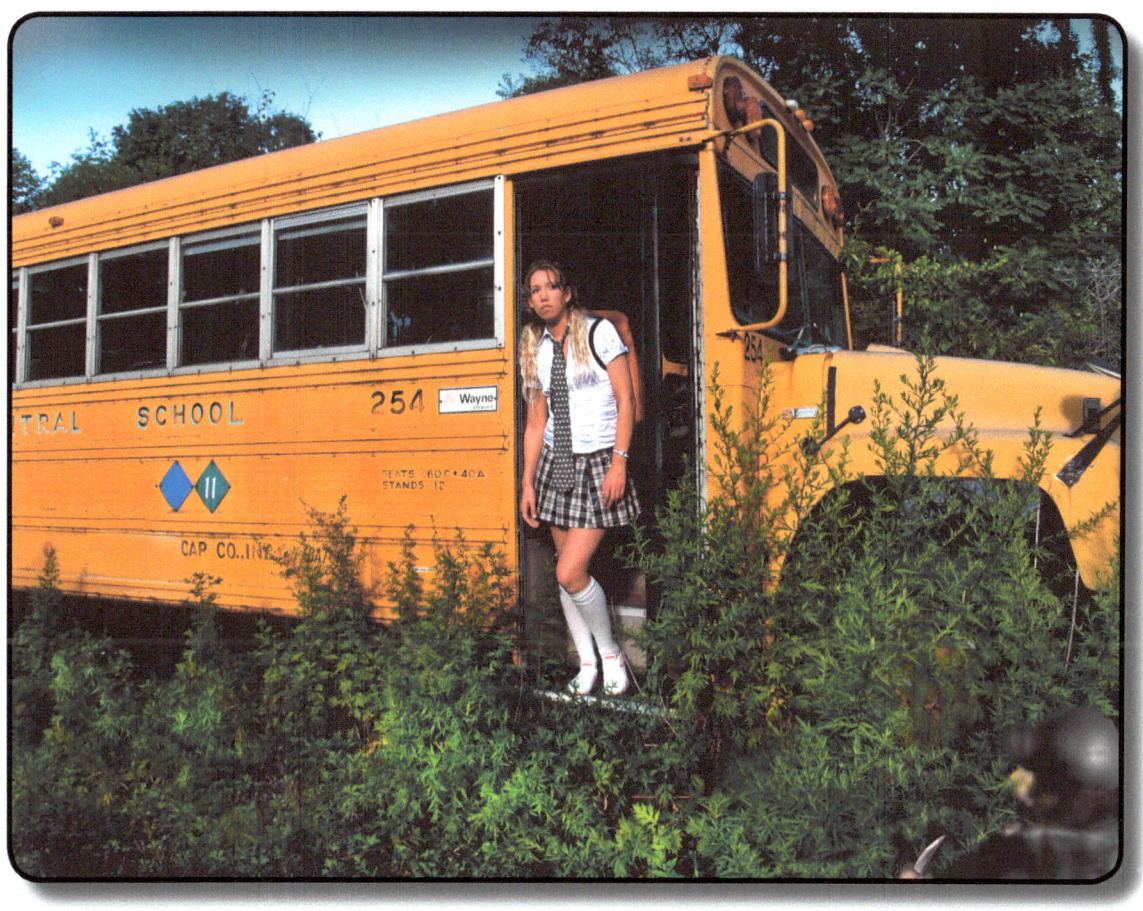

It was definitely a dead end street

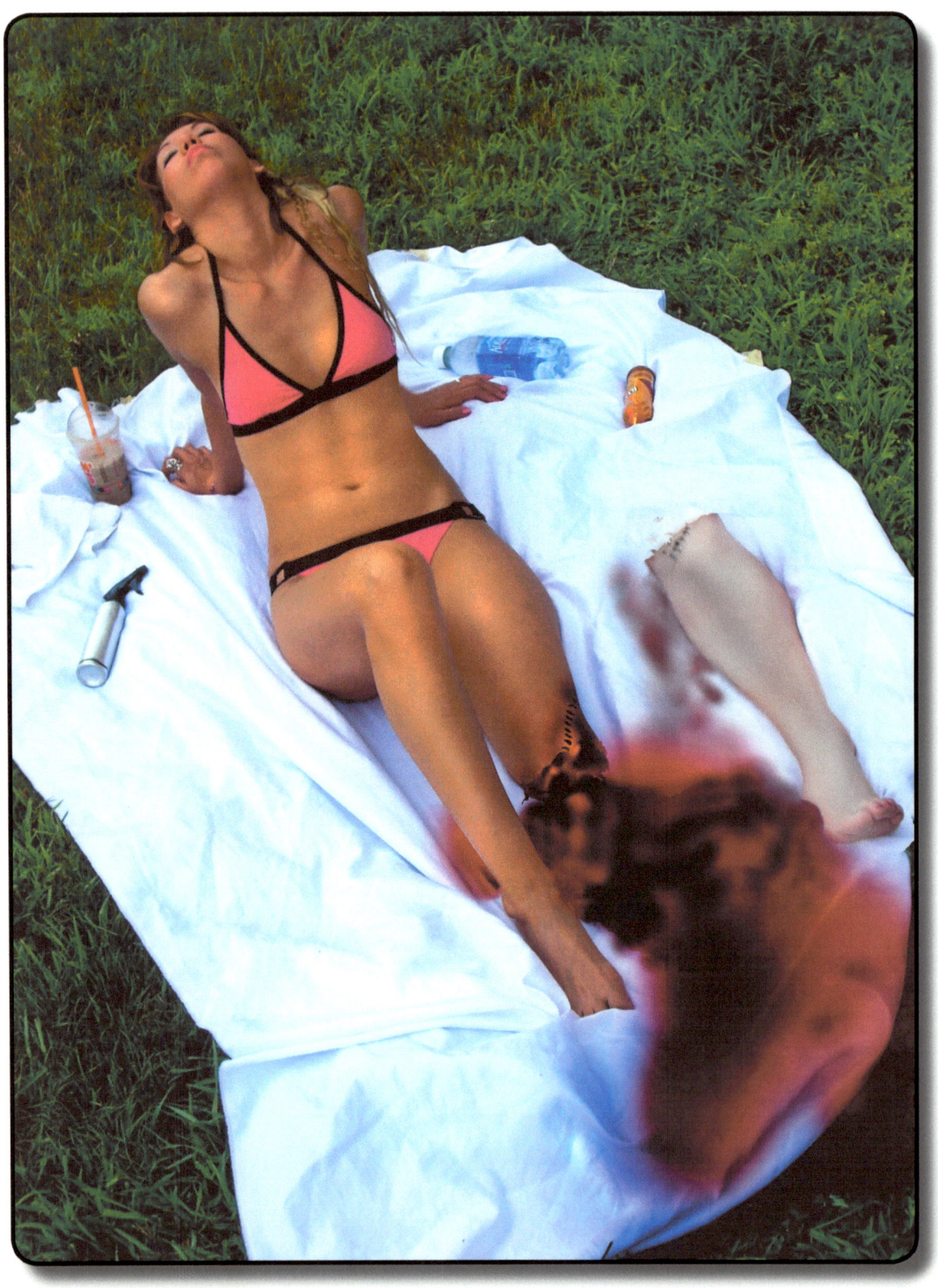

Having suffered a shark attack is still not an excuse to
disregard UV consumption while sunbathing

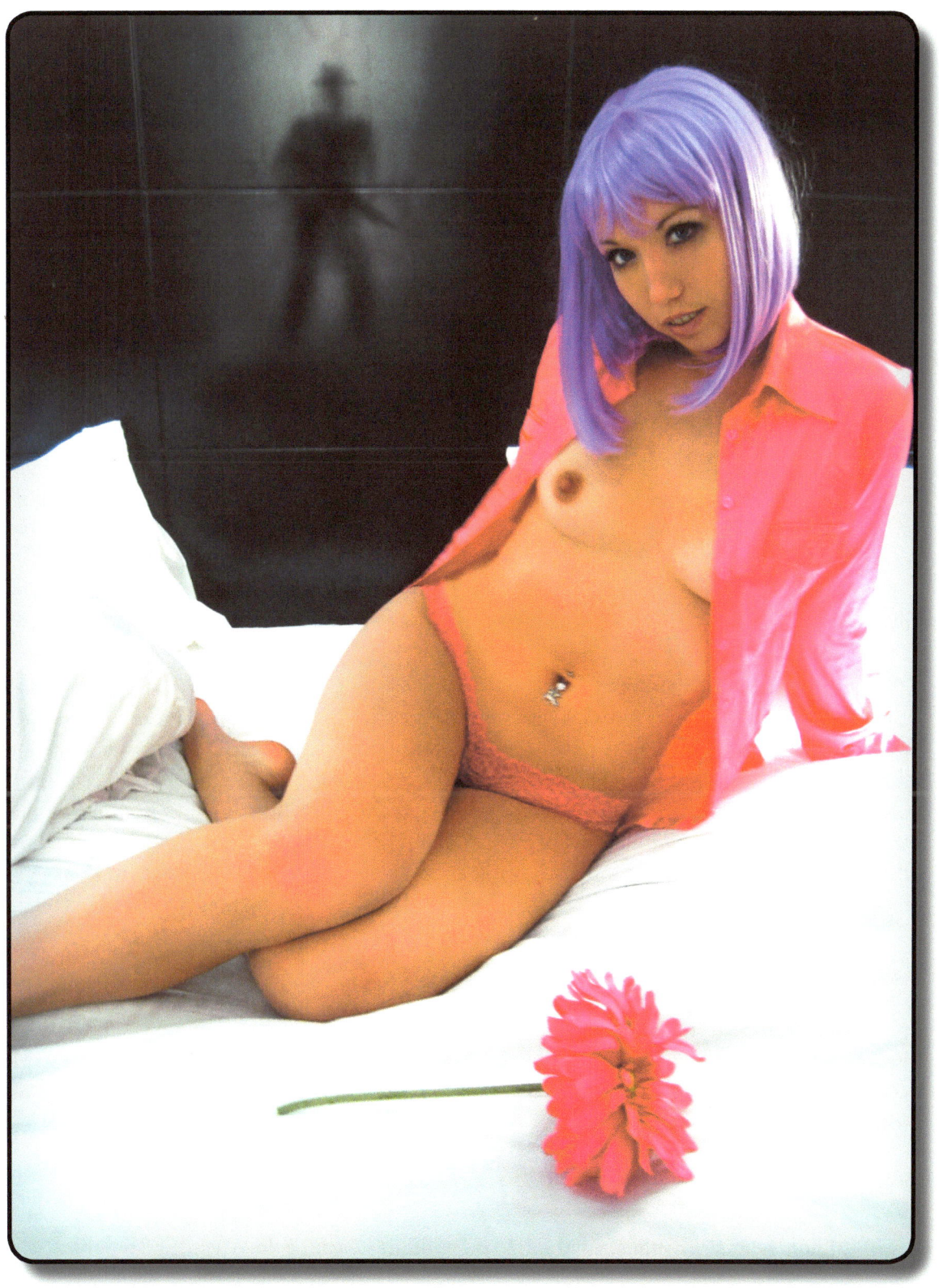

It was a surprise when Bob showed up with the machine gun at midnight

An Interview with Alane Deviare

I had agreed to meet Alane at a little family owned delicatessen in Manhattan Beach, which is just a few minutes from LAX. It was in a small strip mall next to a washateria, and I had heard that they make a pretty tasty hot pastrami on rye. She was about twenty minutes late, and I was desperately trying to resist the temptation to order a sandwich…when I spotted her walking through the door and straight towards my table. [I really meant to edit this into something coherent, but I finally decided to present it here just the way our meeting went.]

"You're late," I said.

"'Sorry - you know how the traffic in LA can be…besides, I'm not late…a 'temptress' arrives exactly when she wants to."

She certainly looked like a temptress to these male eyes: dressed in a pair of VERY short shorts and a "Just Love Me" T-shirt (and I'm pretty sure she was not wearing a bra).

"I'm terrible with small talk and I have a plane to catch in about an hour and a half, so why don't we just go ahead and start...what's this about you having a fear of being upside down?"

"Who told you about that? Did Peter tell you that?" She was laughing. This was my first glimpse of her wonderful smile - she has one of those that really lights up a room. "That actually used to be true! When I was very young, I was really afraid of it. I remember someone holding me upside down and me screaming - so I was scared of it from then on. As I grew older, I learned to love amusement parks and eventually I actually wanted to go on the rides that went upside down. At first, I kept my eyes tightly closed when the roller coaster did flips, then one day (like when I was in high school) I forced myself to open my eyes and I've never looked back since."

"I was also so terrified of sharks when I was a kid…I would JUMP from my bed 'cause I thought they were under it! It all started after I saw *Jaws* when I was all of 4 years old. I remember they used to have the marathons with all the sequels, too. I couldn't even drink red Kool-Aid because I thought it looked like blood! Then I finally decided to watch Shark Week one time and my fear turned into fascination. Now, going into a shark cage is at the top of my Bucket List!"

"What do you like to do for fun?"

"I like skiing, horseback-riding, anything to do with the beach or the ocean, and anything that involves latex or leather!"

"Uh, could you elaborate on that last part?"

"No."

"What is the proudest achievement of your life so far?"

"Not so long ago, I decided to leave upstate New York - where I grew up - to follow my dream of becoming an actress. So...I packed up my stuff and moved to LA all by myself - driving cross country in a U-Haul truck, towing my car behind it. It was an awesome experience! I'm so glad I finally did it!"

"When did you realize that you wanted to be an actress?"

"When I was about 3, I saw the Wizard of Oz. I idolized Judy Garland after that, and I've wanted to be an actress just like her ever since."

"How's that going - the 'trying to become an actress' thing?"

"'Pursuing my dreams still. I've been part of several smaller productions: a stage play, plus some videos and 'shorts'. I'm hoping to get into some bigger productions of course. As they say: 'Never give up your dreams.'"

"Tell me about your experiences working with Peter Manik on *Glamour Horror.*"

"I've known Peter for a long time - he's amazing! It's fun to work with him because our creative minds feed off of each other. We've talked for quite some time about doing a book of images that would encompass both Horror and Glamour, since both of us are such fans of the two genres. It was a lot of fun coming up with the story lines for the photos. Peter is a great director and can always envision just how he wants a scene to be. I'm always amazed when I see the shots we've done - he always knows when he's captured a concept perfectly, and it only takes him maybe 3 shots to get there. He planned every detail of the book, and was really the brains behind it. Peter is an artistic genius. I am so thankful to have him as my co-author, photographer and friend. He has made me the model I am today and I am eternally grateful."

"What kinds of music do you like?"

"Wow - you're really all over the place, aren't you? Uh, I like all kinds of music - music is my life! My parents were hippies and took me to Grateful Dead concerts - and the concerts of a ton of other groups - when I was a kid. I was really into oldies and Elvis and then R&B… then I discovered the Beatles and got hooked on rock. Everclear and Cake are my second and third favorite bands of all time. I really like the new Alternative and Indie rock that is out there now."

"What kinds of things get on your last nerve?"

"Rules, restrictive clothing and mean people."

"Uh, could you elaborate on that middle part?"

"No."

"Okay - it's 'Lightning Round' time! What would you most like to change about yourself?"

"Bigger boobs."

"Best part about being a woman?"

"Multiple orgasms!"

"Worst part?"

"Buying tampons!"

"Favorite season?"

"Summer!! 'Love the beach!"

"Favorite comfort food?"

"Peanut butter and honey on bread."

"Favorite movie?"

"Uh…Rocky Horror Picture Show, Moulin Rouge, Chicago and The Wizard of Oz. I love movies!"

"Heroes in your life?"

"Princess Diana, Marilyn Monroe, and Jane Russell."

"What is there that no one else knows about you?"

"If I told you, then everyone would eventually find out and I couldn't have that!"

"Alane, it's been a distinct pleasure and a privilege talking with you today. I wish you the best of luck in all your pursuits…but I've got a plane to catch. Bye - take care!"

Then I got caught in a traffic jam and missed my flight anyway.

- B. Rubble

An Interview with Peter Manik

Peter had agreed to let me interview him at his studio, located a bit north of New York City. I knocked on his door at the time we had arranged and was greeted by a very attractive female peering through a partially opened door.

"You must be Mr. Rubble - I'm Peter's assistant. 'Just a minute...Peter...Mr. Rubble is here...is it okay if he comes in while you're still shooting?" I heard a male voice asking someone in the room if it was okay with her, then an affirmative reply.

The lovely assistant said "Come on in."

As I walked in, I saw Peter holding a camera up to his face and pointing it at a naked woman. Well, actually, I think she was wearing some lipstick.

"Come in - welcome to my studio...make yourself comfortable. We're running just a little long, but we're almost finished."

I stood there and nodded. Within about ten seconds, it occurred to me that I was more uncomfortable standing there than the unclothed model was. I watched as they completed taking a few more photos, then she gave Peter a peck on the check and smiled at me on her way into another room (to get dressed I supposed).

"Come, come - let's sit down and I'll tell you whatever it is that you want to know."

We sat down and I immediately asked my first question. I don't like to waste time with small talk.

"What's the main focus of your photography these days?"

"For the joy of doing it, I've always liked glamour photography - especially with individuals who are not really model types. Actually, the majority of the people I shoot are not 'model types'. I like the challenge of proving that basically anyone can look like a star - you know, because well - everyone deserves to feel that way."

"That was the basic idea for the "Hamilton Dream Launch" that I did in Canada, with my Canadian associate, Julie Christine. We reached out to everyday regular women and encouraged them to participate in a series of glamour sessions to prove that they are as beautiful as any magazine cover star."

"A big part of what I've been doing for a while now though has been to create solo images and series of images that deal with issues we all see every day in society. 'Could be issues about morality, or correctness or religion or just the societal standards we find today that seem so fake or ridiculous when you look at them real closely. Society is very interesting to me... how the people shape it and how it shapes the people. I like to use my art to point out - to highlight if you will - how false some parts of our society have become. It's a way for me to get my opinions out there."

"So how did you get started photographing all these beautiful women, Peter?"

"I really don't judge anyone as 'beautiful' or 'ugly'. For example, I think I am pretty good looking because of how I look at the world...but then when I look in my bathroom mirror...well, not so super, just average." He laughed as he said that last part.

"Oh I don't know Peter - I'm sure lots of women would say you're a pretty handsome guy!" I said with a big grin on my face.

"Ha! But I thank you anyway Mr. Rubble. I shoot everybody - male, female - doesn't matter how they look. Everyone has some beauty somewhere in them. Have you ever heard a mother say 'oh my kid looks so horrendous...he is plain ugly'? No - mothers see the beauty in their children...and so do I."

"Your models seem to love you, Peter. I heard it when I spoke with Alane, and I just saw it in the eyes of the model you were photographing a few minutes ago. What's your secret?"

Peter laughed. "Oh, I don't have any secret. Of course, I do think they all love me - or at least like me. I certainly hope they do, because if they don't...why would they want to shoot with me, or even spend time with me?"

"I learned this phrase a long time ago: 'I yam who I yam'. If they like who I yam...that's enough for art to develop. You should just look at my paintings or photographs, and like them or don't please. Thank you!"

"Speaking of your paintings - I've seen several and I love them. They are so beautiful! Where does the inspiration for your painting come from?"

"I don't know if my paintings are beautiful or not, because that is quite a personal opinion. All

I know is - I just paint the visions that come to my mind in relation to the subject and theme I do. Since my themes are usually abstract like 'evolution' or 'disintegration' or 'love'…I naturally use my dreams or imagination to create the figures and shapes in the frame as well as the matching colors."

"So what do you enjoy more…painting or photography…and why?"

"I do enjoy both equally. The only difference is the process of creation, which is way faster in the photographic approach than in painting. The preparation for an image might be longer in photography - set design…location choice…equipment…legal papers and permits…props and models…outfits and makeup…all for actually ONE good click. With painting - you are facing a big empty canvas…and you are on your own."

"Advance buzz on *GlamourHorror* has been very positive. It looks like you and Alane were on to something. How was Alane to work with?"

"Alane is a real 'trooper' as they say. She is so upbeat…so full of ideas and energy! She stands up for her friends and loved ones. She isn't scared of anyone - she's absolutely fearless! She crossed this big country alone…drove a rented U-Haul truck all by herself from New York to Hollywood, where she's trying to make her mark now.

"What projects are you working on now?"

"I don't want to bore you about my projects I'm working on. There is no 'artistic calendar' - only 'due dates' and 'plan ideas'. When these two things finally work together, I will be fine." He laughed as he said that.

"Seriously, I am working on my backlog of ideas…trying to put together a great number of the pictures I've shot in the last two years into some kind of coherent 'scheme'. It's one thing to shoot a photo, but it's even more important how you present it. I'm afraid I'm not always so good with the presentation part."

"What's the most important thing in life to you?

"Family, love, health…luck…insurance and taxes…oh, and a good vintage Bentley or custom Lamborghini. I am very simple man after all." There was a twinkle in his eyes.

"And I hope to do many new series with my perfect art partner, Alane…to help shape society."

We talked on for another two hours or so…about just about anything and everything you can think of…but I think I'm going to end this piece here. Let's just say that the last two hours of our conversation were "off the record."

- B. Rubble

About the Author/Photographer: Peter Manik

Peter Manik fell in love with painting while studying architecture in Europe. After moving to America, he earned two college diplomas, one of them in the Fine Art field.

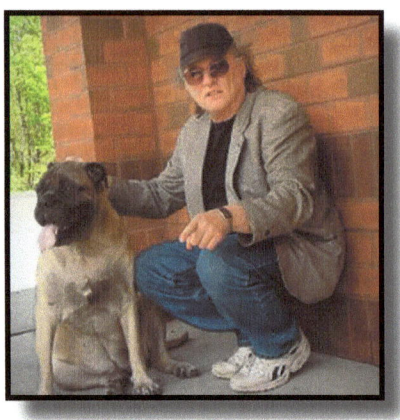

Since earning his Professional Photography Diploma in New York City, Peter's work has appeared in national publications, magazines and books. His naturally charismatic, outgoing personality has brought him many friends, including several celebrities he's worked with. Clients always find it very easy to trust his ability and enthusiastic style.

Peter specializes in Fine Art and Glamour, and likes to sum up his approach to his work and his life with his personal motto:

Live and Let Live. Love and Let Love.

About the Author/Model: Alane Deviare

Alane Deviare is an aspiring actress who started modeling in New York. Growing up in Upstate New York, she knew her whole life that she wanted to be an actress - but was often persecuted for her aspirations. In 2009, tired of trying to do what everyone else wanted, she packed up all her worldly possessions and moved to Hollywood to follow her dreams.

She currently lives in California where she continues to pursue her acting and modeling career, participating in several new and innovative projects.

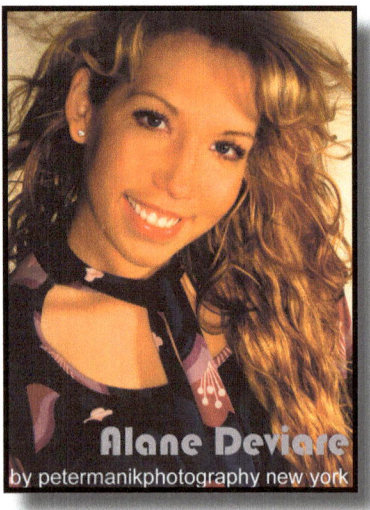

Alane Deviare
by petermanikphotography new york

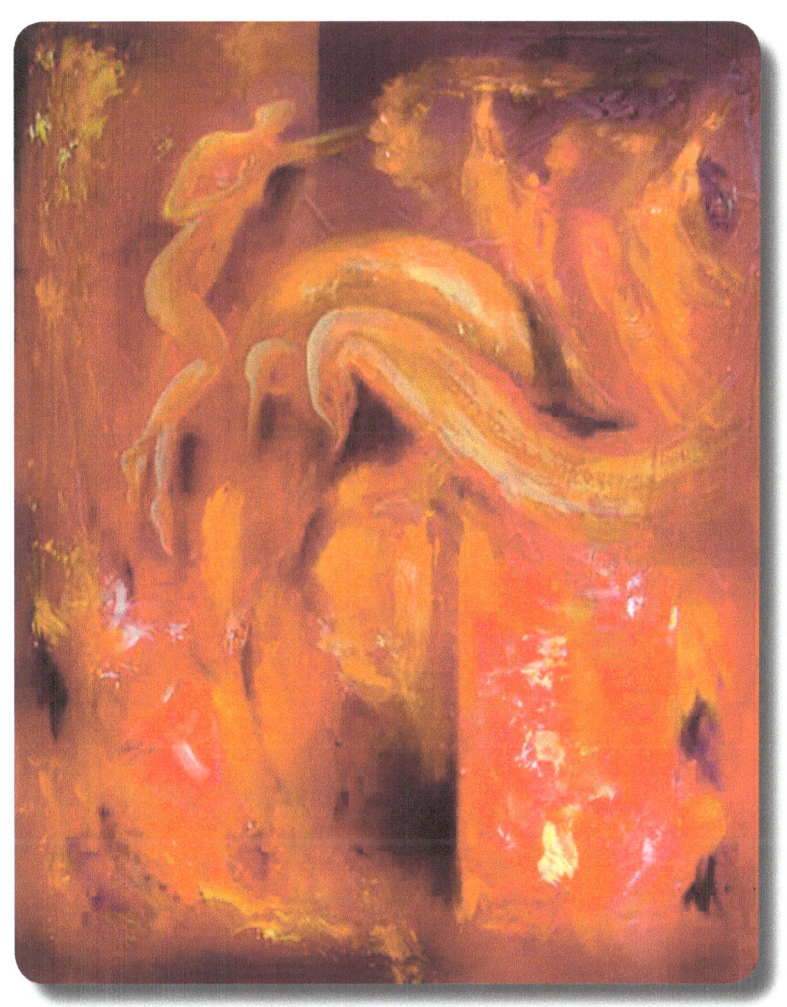

Disintegration #2

A painting by Peter Manik